W9-DBE-795

Past Masters

General Editor   Keith Thomas

Durkheim

Frank Parkin is the author of *Marxism and
Class Theory: A Bourgeois Critique*, *Max Weber*, and
'Peter Rabbit and the *Grundrisse*'.

Past Masters

AQUINAS Anthony Kenny
ARISTOTLE Jonathan Barnes
ARNOLD Stefan Collini
AUGUSTINE Henry Chadwick
BACH Denis Arnold
FRANCIS BACON Anthony Quinton
BAYLE Elisabeth Labrousse
BENTHAM John Dinwiddy
BERGSON Leszek Kolakowski
BERKELEY J. O. Urmson
THE BUDDHA Michael Carrithers
BURKE C. B. Macpherson
CARLYLE A. L. Le Quesne
CERVANTES P. E. Russell
CHAUCER George Kane
CLAUSEWITZ Michael Howard
COBBETT Raymond Williams
COLERIDGE Richard Holmes
CONFUCIUS Raymond Dawson
DANTE George Holmes
DARWIN Jonathan Howard
DESCARTES Tom Sorell
DIDEROT Peter France
GEORGE ELIOT Rosemary Ashton
ENGELS Terrell Carver
ERASMUS James McConica
FREUD Anthony Storr
GALILEO Stillman Drake
GIBBON J. W. Burrow
GOETHE T. J. Reed
HEGEL Peter Singer
HOBBES Richard Tuck
HOMER Jasper Griffin
HUME A. J. Ayer

KIERKEGAARD Patrick Gardiner
JESUS Humphrey Carpenter
KANT Roger Scruton
LAMARCK L. J. Jordanova
LEIBNIZ G. MacDonald Ross
LOCKE John Dunn
MACHIAVELLI Quentin Skinner
MALTHUS Donald Winch
MARX Peter Singer
MENDEL Vitezslav Orel
MILL William Thomas
MONTAIGNE Peter Burke
MONTESQUIEU Judith N. Shklar
THOMAS MORE Anthony Kenny
WILLIAM MORRIS Peter Stansky
MUHAMMAD Michael Cook
NEWMAN Owen Chadwick
PAINE Mark Philp
PASCAL Alban Krailsheimer
PAUL E. P. Sanders
PETRARCH Nicholas Mann
PLATO R. M. Hare
PROUST Derwent May
RUSKIN George P. Landow
SCHILLER T. J. Reed
SCHOPENHAUER Christopher Janaway
SHAKESPEARE Germaine Greer
ADAM SMITH D. D. Raphael
SPINOZA Roger Scruton
TOLSTOY Henry Gifford
VICO Peter Burke
VIRGIL Jasper Griffin
WITTGENSTEIN A. C. Grayling
WYCLIF Anthony Kenny

Forthcoming

JOSEPH BUTLER R. G. Frey
COPERNICUS Owen Gingerich
GODWIN Alan Ryan
JOHNSON Pat Rogers
JUNG Anthony Stevens
LINNAEUS W. T. Stearn

NEWTON P. M. Rattansi
ROUSSEAU Robert Wokler
RUSSELL Anthony Grayling
SOCRATES Bernard Williams
TOCQUEVILLE Larry Siedentop
MARY WOLLSTONECRAFT
    William St Clair
and others

Frank Parkin

DURKHEIM

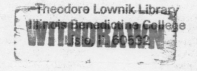
Oxford   New York
OXFORD UNIVERSITY PRESS
1992

Oxford University Press, Walton Street, Oxford OX2 6DP

Oxford New York Toronto
Delhi Bombay Calcutta Madras Karachi
Petaling Jaya Singapore Hong Kong Tokyo
Nairobi Dar es Salaam Cape Town
Melbourne Auckland

and associated companies in
Berlin Ibadan

First published 1992 as an Oxford University Press paperback

British Library Cataloguing in Publication Data
Data available
ISBN 0-19-287672-4

Library of Congress Cataloging in Publication Data
Parkin, Frank.
    Durkheim/Frank Parkin.
        p.   cm. — (Past masters)
    Includes bibliographical references and index.
    1. Durkheim, Emile, 1858-1917. 2. Sociology—France—History.
    I. Title.   II. Series.
    301'.092—dc20   HM22.F8D8687 1992 92-7787
    ISBN 0-19-287672-4 (pbk.)

Typeset by Best-set Typesetter Ltd., Hong Kong
Printed in Great Britain by
Biddles Ltd.
Guildford and King's Lynn

To Harry

Contents

Note on abbreviations

The following abbreviations are used in references given in the text:

D	*The Division of Labour in Society*
Da	Davy, 'Émile Durkheim: L'Homme'
Do	Douglas, *The Social Meanings of Suicide*
Du	*Durkheim on Religion* (ed. Pickering)
E	*Durkheim: Essays on Morals and Education* (ed. Pickering)
F	*Les Formes élémentaires de la vie religieuse*
Fr	Frazer, *The Golden Bough*
G	*Durkheim on Politics and the State* (ed. Giddens)
I	'Individualism and the Intellectuals'
J	Jones, *Émile Durkheim*
L	*Leçons de sociologie*
Lk	Lukes, *Émile Durkheim: His Life and Work*
Lu	Lukes, 'Introduction' to *Rules*
M	Marx, *Capital*, vol. iii
Ma	Marx, *Grundrisse*
ME	*Moral Education*
MER	Marx and Engels, *On Religion*
MR	*Montesquieu and Rousseau*
P	*Primitive Classification*
R	*Rules of Sociological Method*
S	*Le Suicide*
SSS	*Socialism and Saint-Simon*
T	'Two Laws of Penal Evolution'

Full bibliographic details of these and other works are given in the suggestions for further reading at the end of the book.

Background

Durkheim presents us with something of a conundrum. He is almost universally acclaimed as a social theorist of the very first rank, a writer whose works easily bear comparison with those of Marx and Weber, and whose ideas have had a profound and lasting impact on sociology. Yet at the same time, few if any of the theories he espoused on such diverse matters as the foundations of social order, the causes of suicide, the origin and functions of religion, the evolution of law, the nature of property, and the role and character of the modern state, would meet with the endorsement of those who hold him in such high regard. Sociologists calling themselves Durkheimians are extremely difficult to find, whereas self-styled Marxists and Weberians are everywhere in evidence.

One possible explanation for this is that Durkheim has made his presence felt more by virtue of the kinds of questions he asked than by the answers he gave to them. And, as every graduate student in search of a thesis topic knows, it requires more creative effort to pose the appropriate problem than to come up with a solution. Sociologists might well have rejected Durkheim's answers, but they continue to wrestle with the questions he raised and to plunder the Aladdin's cave of concepts that he bequeathed. He had a remarkable facility for standing at a tangent to society and seeing its commonplace features with a Martian's eye. To read him on any topic, be it ever so familiar, is never to think of it in quite the same way again. A sociology shorn of its Durkheimian preoccupations and idiom would be a lacklustre thing.

His contribution to the discipline is likely to be raised even higher in esteem now that Marxism has passed its heyday and seems set to slide into terminal decline. Sociology is not endowed with an impressive pantheon of intellectual founders, and the depletion of Marx's legacy will result in Weber and Durkheim having to bear an even greater burden than before. The recent closure of the East European laboratories of applied Marxism could be expected to give a fillip to Durkheim's sociology in another respect. Much of his scholarly effort was aimed at finding a solution to what he felt to be the most pressing problem of his day, a problem which is essentially the same as that facing post-socialist regimes: namely, how to realign the foundations of social order in a system afflicted with 'anomy'. This is a condition in which the old moral order has fallen into decay and a new one has yet to emerge in its place. Durkheim argued that in this normative vacuum, the latent forces of chaos would thrive and multiply, unchecked by any internal constraints. Although disaster could only be kept at bay through the aid of a new moral consensus, this in turn presupposed a root-and-branch reform of the system of distributive justice. The trouble was, there was no guarantee that the necessary reforms would be put in place in sufficient time.

Durkheim's acute sensitivity to the possibilities of anarchy is often attributed to the turbulence of the period in which he lived. There is perhaps something in this, though not a great deal. He was born in 1858 in Épinal, an otherwise undistinguished town in Lorraine. He was still a schoolboy at the time of France's defeat in the Franco-Prussian war and the ensuing Paris Commune. While he would certainly have witnessed occupying troops lording it over the locals, it hardly follows that the events of 1870–1 would of themselves have set his mind working in a direction from which it never subsequently veered. People respond to the same political stimuli in different ways and interpret them in the light of their own moral disposition. In any case, Durkheim's career coincided with the Third Republic, a period of relative tranquillity judged by the standards of the revolutionary past. The Republic was, to be sure, riddled by animosities between the Church and anticlericals, Monarchists and Republicans, animosities which occasionally came to a head, as they did most notably in the Dreyfus affair. But squabbles of this kind are common to most societies for much of the time, and a society whose principal battleground was the Dreyfus scandal could count itself fortunate.

It is very likely that Durkheim's concern with the problem of social order was shaped more by his immersion in the ideas of Saint-Simon and Comte than by what was happening in the streets. Many of the themes that he pursued, and the rules of method that he advocated, are directly traceable to the writings of his two immediate predecessors. Although few sociologists would wish to deny the impress of Saint-Simon and Comte on Durkheim's cast of thought, there is some lively disagreement about the relative influence of the two thinkers. Those who portray Durkheim as a man of the Left are inclined to stress his affiliation to Saint-Simon, the founder of Utopian socialism, and to play down his links with Comte, the 'mad philosopher'. Those who see him as an essentially conservative theorist tend to put the emphasis the other way, highlighting in particular his own readiness to acknowledge his debt to Comtean positivism.

It says something for the complexity of Durkheim's thought that it could so confidently be assigned to opposite poles of the political spectrum. He has at one time or another been dubbed a socialist, a syndicalist, a radical, a liberal, a conservative, and even a proto-Fascist. No one has yet detected a streak of anarchism in his make-up, but the possibility should not be ruled out. At the practical level he was none of these things, since he had a dim view of political activity and quite properly believed that he could exercise more sway over events through his teaching and his writings than by manning notional barricades. The one occasion on which he was persuaded to set aside his books and enter the political fray was at the height of the Dreyfus case. But although he was an active Dreyfusard it is altogether characteristic that his celebrated article on the affair should read less like a defence of the accused man than an advertisement for his novel theory of moral individualism.

In 1879 he entered the *École normale supérieure*, having had three bites of the cherry before satisfying the examiners. Now in his early twenties, he chafed at first against the schoolboy diet of Latin exercises and what he felt to be the pervasive air of sloppy humanism (Da 185). This was hardly the preparation likely to commend itself to someone already imbued with a scientific outlook. Things improved in his second and third years and in later life he looked back on his time at the school with some affection, experiencing the kind of pleasure that is only enjoyed in retrospect. He was by all accounts a skilled dialectician and was held in considerable awe by his fellow *normaliens* on account of his professorial style. He was also extremely strait-laced, not the sort to indulge in undergraduate larks or to harbour improper thoughts of hanky-panky. This air of solemnity hung over him all his life, so that even to his closest colleagues he could seem a rather forbidding figure. It is not easy to picture Durkheim relaxing over a drink or laughing aloud at something funny, other than Herbert Spencer.

He took his *agrégation* in 1882, coming bottom of the class but one. He then followed the common practice of teaching in a *lycée* in what amounted to a kind of apprenticeship for an academic or professional career. After three years of this he was sent on leave to Germany as one of a number of young scholars charged with the official duty of investigating and reporting on German universities. This policy was inspired by the French government's belief that the secret of the enemy's military prowess was encoded in its system of higher education. Durkheim arrived in Berlin on his mission of academic espionage in 1885. Weber was also in Berlin in that year, pursuing his law studies, but it is unlikely that the two young men would have brushed shoulders on the Unter den Linden, because just as Durkheim was arriving, Weber was leaving for Göttingen. The timing might almost have been deliberate, for not only did the two luminaries never once meet or correspond, they even contrived to turn a blind eye to one another's publications. Each was familiar with the other's language and much of its sociological literature, but neither gave any sign of familiarity with the other's ideas. It was as if there was a mutual recognition that a fruitful dialogue would be impossible given the wholly incompatible methods and assumptions on which their respective sociologies were based.

Not long after returning from Germany, Durkheim was rewarded with a teaching post in social science and education at the University of Bordeaux. His fifteen years at Bordeaux (1887–1902) proved to be a period of high creativity and Stakhanovite endeavour. Three of his books, *The Division of Labour in Society*, *The Rules of Sociological Method*, and *Suicide*, were published at this time in addition to a dazzling array of articles on law, religion, incest prohibition, and totemism. It was at Bordeaux that he founded and edited the *Année sociologique*, arguably the most influential journal ever produced in the social sciences, and the vehicle through which he and his collaborators articulated the principles of a distinctive school of sociology. He also found time to marry Louise Dreyfus (no relation to the unfortunate army captain) and to have two children by her.

In 1902 he received what every French provincial academic openly or secretly prays for: the summons to Paris. He was appointed to a post in education at the Sorbonne, later converted to a Chair. In those early days sociology had to be taught under the guise of something more acceptable to academic convention, rather in the way that, more than half a century later, it had to be smuggled into Oxford under the skirts of politics. Durkheim was already a controversial figure when he arrived in Paris, and almost before he had unpacked he was subjected to an extraordinary barrage of personal vituperation. His adversaries, drawn largely from the Catholic Right, portrayed him as the new Antichrist, an inspirationally evil propagandist bent on poisoning young minds with his aggressive secularism and his crackpot science of sociology—which was merely a fancy name for socialism anyway. They found it monstrous that someone of Durkheim's views should occupy such a powerful position in the educational system, responsible as he was for shaping the ideas and attitudes of the nation's schoolteachers. Durkheim stood up well under fire and might even have relished the controversy. To be anathematized by men whose commitment to the Republic and the values of liberal democracy was, at best, equivocal must have reassured him that he was on the right track.

During his tenure in Paris he used his growing influence within educational circles to secure the position of sociology as an independent discipline and to advance the fortunes of his own lieutenants. The latter, easily identifiable through their association with the *Année sociologique*, were conspicuously more successful in winning university and research posts than competitors who had not been admitted to the Durkheimian *nomenklatura*. The master was not famous for his toleration of other schools of thought, and the accusations of empire-building that were sometimes levelled against him were not too wide of the mark. But what to those on the outside might look like academic imperialism could be seen by the insiders as single-mindedness of purpose, a total commitment and dedication to the cause of sociology, without which it would have foundered.

Durkheim did undoubtedly pursue his goal with the verve and passion of a holy crusader. Georges Davy, a member of his inner circle, recalled that listening to him lecture was like being in the presence 'of a prophet of some nascent religion' (Da 194). Durkheim was descended from a long line of rabbis and had contemplated following the same path. His change of mind was all to the good. Judaism is not a proselytizing religion and would not have satisfied his missionary urge in the way that sociology was able to. He was, like Weber, a non-believer fascinated by religion and devoted the best part of his mature years to the study of its supposedly simplest forms. References to religion are peppered throughout his early works, but it was not until 1895 that, on his own reckoning, its full sociological import really dawned upon him. In that year he underwent a sudden 'revelation' (R 259). What happened? He did not see an apparition or hear celestial voices; he encountered the writings of Robertson Smith, an anthropologist who, unusually for that time, interpreted religious beliefs and practices as part of the social matrix and no different in principle from other cultural products. Durkheim's fertile imagination seized upon this idea and fashioned it into an elaborate design that was unmistakably his own. The result was *The Elementary Forms of the Religious Life* (1912), his most brilliant and unsettling work, a book destined to have the same impact on its readers that Smith's book had had on him.

It was mainly through his writings on religion that he first caught the attention of foreign scholars. Although it was the last of his books, *Elementary Forms* was the first to be translated into English; all the others were translated posthumously. His ideas were little known in this country or the United States during his own lifetime, in contrast to the present state of affairs in which the latest intellectual fashions from Paris are avidly snapped up by the more impressionable minds on this side of the Channel. In France itself, his influence fell into decline after the First World War. Many of his intimate colleagues, his son among them, did not return from the trenches. He himself died, in 1917, from one of those vague illnesses brought on by a combination of exhaustion and melancholy. The *Année* continued to be published, but it was never quite the same without its guiding spirit.

After the Second World War, Durkheim's writings found a

much wider readership. While there has been no renaissance of the Durkheimian school as such, his teachings have enjoyed a new lease of life following the exponential growth in the social sciences in the heady days of university expansion. His reputation internationally stands higher today than ever before and is unlikely to diminish. No one wholly unfamiliar with his ideas could now claim to have a fully rounded education. In the following pages I have tried to set out these ideas in plain language, less by way of exegesis than in the form of a critical commentary. It goes without saying that a book of this length cannot pretend to be the last word on the subject; and it is certainly no substitute for the texts themselves. All that it can really hope to do is to whet the reader's appetite for a taste of the real thing.

1 Sociology as science

I

'All science would be superfluous if the outward appearance and the essence of things directly coincided.' (Ma 817) Marx's dictum could easily have been coined by Durkheim. Both men held that the world of mere appearances—social reality as immediately perceived—was more of a mirage than a solid factual entity. Capitalism for Marx and Society for Durkheim were mysterious affairs which could not be apprehended by means of received ideas and plain observations. Genuine understanding came only by penetrating beneath the surface of things to reach the hidden essence. To accomplish this, the seeker after truth had to be armed with a battery of concepts custom-made for the task, concepts which owed nothing to the tissue of illusions otherwise known as common sense.

Marx may have felt that such a muscular intellectual effort was called for only to reveal the arcane secrets of capitalism, a system that was made more than ordinarily obscure by the mists of bourgeois ideology. Durkheim, for his part, believed that society of almost any stamp was unknown territory, not least of all to the people who comprised it. Ideology as such was not the problem; the obstruction to understanding was really to do with the use of layman's concepts instead of more rigorous, scientific ones. Durkheim's remedy was not to propose a series of neologisms but to redefine common-or-garden concepts and give them a fresh meaning unique to himself. This strategy was well suited to his methodological shock-tactics of stating propositions designed to subvert everyday assumptions. Durkheim often seemed to operate under the conviction that any argument or thesis which flew in the face of common sense was thereby endowed with scientific status.

The extent of the gulf that he felt existed between lay ideas and a science of society is revealed most clearly in his remarkable treatise, *The Rules of Sociological Method* (1895). To lay down firm rules for the conduct of research might be considered a rash thing to do. It is simply an invitation to critics to show how the author of the rules has flouted them in the course of empirical enquiry. Such a charge has sometimes been levelled against Durkheim, though in fact he remained quite faithful to the main tenets of his manifesto throughout his subsequent work. That is half the trouble with it.

The leitmotif running through the *Rules* is that the facts of social life are no different in principle from facts about the physical universe. The methods employed in the study of the latter are therefore wholly applicable to the study of the former. Durkheim's stance is summed up in his famous and cryptic injunction 'to consider social facts as things' (R 60). It is not immediately apparent what this actually requires us to do, nor how it would differ from considering facts as something other than things. But of course Durkheim is using the word 'thing' in his own private way. A thing is 'any object of knowledge which is not naturally penetrable by the understanding' (R 36). It is some aspect of reality that we cannot grasp and comprehend by dint of intuition or reflection. Things have the quality of existing independently of the ideas used in understanding them, rather in the way that apples fall from a tree without benefit of the concept of gravity.

To become a fully fledged science, sociology must abandon its obsession with speculative reasoning and armchair theorizing in favour of factual enquiry. This was intended as a side-swipe at sociologists like Comte and Herbert Spencer, whose grand schemas and elaborate systems were more akin to philosophical musings than to the kind of fine-grained investigations that science demanded. Direct confrontation with the factual world also required the sociologist to cleanse his mind of its accumulated detritus. 'He must free himself from those fallacious notions which hold sway over the mind of the ordinary person, shaking off, once and for all, the yoke of those empirical categories that long habit often makes tyrannical.' (R 73) Durkheim recognized that this act of cerebral hygiene would be less easy for the social scientist than his counterpart in the natural sciences. Studying the reproductive system of the earthworm did not kindle quite the same human passions as the study of religious belief or political behaviour. Nevertheless, the sociologist could, with

9

sufficient effort, subordinate his emotions to the dictates of scholarly objectivity, as he himself was soon to demonstrate in his study of suicide. If such a sensitive subject as this could be tackled with clinical dispassion, the case for the scientific method would more or less be clinched.

Social facts considered as things partook of another important quality, apart from their independence of concepts. Facts could not be called social merely on the grounds that such phenomena arose from human behaviour. On that basis, almost everything that people did would fall under the heading of social, with the consequence that sociology could not lay claim to a distinct subject-matter of its own. Social facts therefore had to be defined more narrowly as 'manners of acting, thinking and feeling external to the individual, which are invested with a coercive power by virtue of which they exercise control over him' (R 52). In other words, facts are social when the activities they refer to are governed by some form or other of constraint.

This turns out to be a fairly elastic definition, since very few human activities could be said to occur completely free of constraint. The threat of physical force, economic sanctions, or moral disapproval all count equally as forms of coercion or constraint on a person's behaviour. For Durkheim there is no difference in principle between the restraining influence of a policeman's baton and an eyebrow cocked in disapproval. The fact that constraints upon behaviour vary a great deal in their severity is seen as less important than the fact that they all share two crucial features: all are backed up by sanctions, and all have their source in collective life.

In the ordinary course of events, we are not generally aware of the extent to which our conduct is subject to forces of constraint. We no more feel the weight of such forces pressing upon us than we feel the pressure of the air. Their presence only becomes fully apparent when we attempt to act in defiance of them. The reaction of others, in the form of the sanctions they impose, serves to reveal the moral boundary we have overstepped, whether wittingly or otherwise. The punishment of crime is the most obvious, if extreme, case of how coercive powers are made manifest by the act of defying them. Despite their apparent differences, normative constraints work in the same way as physical ones.

Durkheim speaks of the coercive power of custom and convention, rules of behaviour which are enforced by the strength of common sentiment. Even trends in fashion are a form of compulsion: 'We can no more choose the design of our houses than the cut of our clothes...the one is as much obligatory as the other.' (R 58) More correctly, we could dress unconventionally if we so chose, but only at the risk of social censure. Durkheim is notionally at liberty to deliver his lectures wearing a grass skirt, but the mere thought of the public ridicule he would have to endure effectively closes off this option.

His enumeration of the myriad ways in which we are seduced, cajoled, and bullied into toeing the line reads like a prelude to the critique of society as a prison-house. Durkheim seems to be on the verge of echoing Rousseau's plaintive cry that man is born free, but is everywhere in chains. But such a bleak assessment could not be further from Durkheim's way of seeing it. Far from enslaving people, social rules and constraints were their saving grace. Without a powerful apparatus of social constraint, egoism would run rampant and orderly life would dissolve into the nightmare of a Hobbesian state of nature.

What made constraint a virtue rather than a vice was the fact that it was a collective thing. For Durkheim, practically everything of social worth and of value to humankind was a product of collective life. Measured by any standard, the collectivity was greatly superior to the individual; it was the fount of all that was best in us, the source of all morality. Each individual made a contribution to the whole, but the resulting synthesis was something much more than the sum of its parts, just as a plum pudding was something over and above the separate ingredients which went into its making.

Collective life generates an emergent property, a form of social consciousness that is altogether different from states of individual consciousness. This so-called *conscience collective*, or common consciousness, is the only valid object of sociological enquiry. Collective forces and representations have a reality *sui generis*; they express a meaning and significance that cannot be reached by way of the individual's state of mind. The latter was the domain of psychology, the former of sociology, two disciplines as different in their subject-matter as chemistry and physics.

Durkheim's contrast between individual and collective phenomena was proclaimed so often and with such insistence that one could easily assume that all the heavy guns of the academic establishment were ranged against him on the issue. In fact his position was not seriously at odds with prevailing opinion. The reason why he stated it in such uncompromising terms was probably bound up with his drive to carve out a niche for sociology in the university system. He needed, or felt that he needed, to demonstrate that the new discipline had a legitimate claim to a territory of its own, one that science had so far left untouched. This is not of course to say that his intellectual stance was merely a ploy or a manœuvre in the intricate game of academic politics. There can be no doubting the strength of his conviction that sociology had a unique contribution to offer and that this lay in the identification of social reality as a product of collective life.

The same might be said of his vision of sociology as a positive science. There was, in any case, nothing particularly eccentric about this. The respect, even awe, in which the natural sciences were held was a notable feature of French intellectual life in general, and had been so since the Enlightenment. Durkheim's immediate predecessors, Saint-Simon and Comte, also had scientific pretensions; he, however, unlike them, sought to realize his aims by the application of scientific method. There was no point in talking about science if one did not also adopt the rigorous procedures of science. Without the use of method, sociology would never get beyond the ramblings of Herbert Spencer and other armchair dilettantes.

Of all the criticisms to which Durkheim's work has been subjected, it is perhaps his attempt to ape the methods of natural science which has aroused most scorn. The modern, or post-modern, era has witnessed a sharp reaction against all shades of positivism and a pooh-poohing of the very idea of a social science. Durkheim was a natural target for the anti-positivist onslaught. His classic study, *Suicide* (1897), has understandably borne the brunt of the attack. Whereas the *Rules* is part manifesto, part statement of intent, *Suicide* is among other things a practical handbook, an illustrated guide to scientific method. It is in this work above all others that the intricate mechanism of Durkheim's reasoning is exposed to full view. This reasoning has been said to be flawed on many counts; some of the objections raised are well founded, while others are less damaging to Durkheim than to his critics. Let us examine the case set out in *Suicide* before turning to its defects, real and supposed.

II

The choice of suicide as a topic for investigation might at first blush seem rather perverse, given Durkheim's commitment to the study of collective behaviour. The taking of one's own life would surely qualify as the quintessentially individual act, one that could only be understood within the framework of human psychology. It was perhaps the apparent inaptness of the topic which made it so attractive to Durkheim. If he could demonstrate the explanatory power of his method on the least promising material, its scientific credentials would be established without further question. It is a measure of his own belief in its validity that he was willing to test it to destruction.

He begins by confronting us with an intriguing puzzle. We are in possession of a remarkable piece of information: we know roughly how many people in France, or in England, will kill themselves this year. And not merely this year, but next year and the year after. We know this because the suicide rate in every country for which there are reliable figures is fairly constant over time. The numbers are bound to fluctuate a little from year to year, but only within a narrow range. The suicide rate is like the rainfall rate; some years are wetter than others, but decade for decade the average is pretty constant.

Now, given that we know in advance roughly how many people in France, or wherever, will kill themselves next year, how could it be maintained that suicide was a purely individual phenomenon? If the suicide rate was nothing more than the sum total of random and unconnected personal acts, we should expect the figures to fluctuate considerably from one year to another. The fact that they do not can hardly be attributed to chance. It puts too much strain on credulity to suppose that each year, purely by coincidence, about the same number of people decide to do away with themselves. The suicide rate even remains stable while the population is changing. Take Paris, for example;

migrations in and out of the city occur unceasingly, yet despite the continuous state of flux, the suicide rate for Paris remains stubbornly constant. Something other than the decisions of individuals must account for this regularity.

A clue as to what this something other might be is offered by the fact that variations in the rate of suicide are found among different groups and localities in the same society. Why, Durkheim asks, should social groups vary systematically in their propensity to suicide? The answer is that every social group has a certain 'collective disposition' to suicide. That is to say, the number of suicides occurring in any given social group is prefigured or programmed in its structure. In Durkheim's words:

> It is the moral constitution of society which fixes at any given time the quota of voluntary deaths. Thus, for every people there exists a collective force of specific power which drives men to kill themselves. The victim's actions which at first sight appear to express nothing but his own disposition are, in fact, the manifestation or external expression of a social condition. (S 336)

Naturally we cannot know in advance who the actual victims will be. But that is not the point. The point is to reveal the nature of the collective forces at work which render some people more vulnerable than others to the suicidal impulse. Durkheim sees society as suffering from a kind of plague which infects people with the urge to self-destruction—the so-called 'suicidogenetic current'. Some categories of the population enjoy a high degree of immunity from the epidemic; others are at much greater risk. It is this differential vulnerability to suicide which Durkheim comes to focus on as the main sociological problem to be explained.

Previous attempts to tackle the problem had often given prominence to the motives for suicide. Durkheim is dismissive of this approach. People kill themselves for a whole variety of reasons: unrequited love, gambling debts, family dishonour, examination failure, bankruptcy—the list is almost endless. Enumerating the motives for suicide gets us nowhere. Besides, the personal anxieties and upsets which may lead people to take their own lives are found among the members of all social groups. The question is, why are the members of some groups better able than others to withstand the calamities of life? Why is it that some people are able to cope with the most appalling personal disasters while others do away with themselves at the smallest misfortune? The recitation of motives cannot answer the question.

Durkheim seeks to show that groups which are prone to suicide have certain social characteristics in common, as do those which are more resistant to it. An impressive array of official statistics is marshalled in support of this claim—the kind of social facts that guaranteed the scientific nature of the enterprise. Moreover, apparently unrelated facts could be arranged in such a way as to reveal an underlying pattern, the stuff of reality not visible to the untutored eye. The evidence showed, among other things, that people who were divorced or widowed had a higher rate of suicide than married people; that city dwellers had a higher rate than villagers; that members of small families had a higher rate than members of large families; that Protestants had a higher rate than Catholics; that the well educated had a higher rate than the uneducated.

Durkheim reasoned that among these pairs, the groups with the lower rate of suicide all shared one thing in common: each was a more cohesive social unit, more of a 'moral community' than its opposite number. People who lived in the bosom of the family or in village communities had a greater anchorage in society than those who lived alone or in big cities. Catholics, similarly, were more close-knit as a religious community than Protestants; Catholics were members of an all-embracing 'mother Church', a collective moral entity that was resistant to the schisms and sectarian divides of Protestant individualism. That was why they were less prone to kill themselves than Protestants. Differences in the suicide rate between the highly educated and the uneducated are explained on similar lines. Higher education encourages a spirit of free enquiry and scepticism; as a result, intellectuals tend to have a weak attachment to the central values and traditional symbols of society. Their isolation is a normative one.

Durkheim concludes from all this that insulation from the suicidal current is best afforded by the bonds of social integration. Members of closely knit groups or cohesive moral communities enjoy the greatest protection; conversely, people who lack social roots or suffer isolation are prime candidates for meeting the suicide quota. Durkheim called this type of suicide 'egoistic', on the grounds that its victims were reliant only upon their own resources, without the support of society. We thus arrive at the proposition that egoistic suicide 'varies in inverse ratio to the degree of integration of the social groups to which the individual belongs' (S 223). The greater the number of well-integrated groups a person belongs to, the better the protection against egoistic suicide.

Immunity against egoistic suicide does not, however, offer *carte blanche* protection. There are other types of suicide that spring from different causes and which call for different prophylactic measures. One of these is 'altruistic' suicide. Altruistic suicide comes about for precisely the opposite reason to egoistic suicide—namely, because the individual is too fully integrated into the group or community. It arises when a person is so immersed in the life of society that he lacks all identity as an individual in his own right. When society is everything, the individual is nothing.

Altruistic suicide is the normal type in simple societies based on mechanical solidarity. A tribal member who, through age or infirmity, feels himself to be a burden on the community may decide to take the customary way out. The fate of one individual is as nothing compared to the survival of the clan. Altruistic suicide is quite rare in more advanced societies, but it does occur, notably among the military. Soldiers, like tribesmen, are required to think of themselves as expendable in the service of a greater good. Suicide under these conditions may express itself in acts of heroism, as in the example of the kamikaze pilot. Instances of this kind fall squarely within Durkheim's overall definition of suicide as 'any case of death which comes about directly or indirectly from a negative or positive act carried out by the victim himself and which he knows is bound to produce this result' (S 5).

Altruistic suicide was a positive act, to be sure, but it was nevertheless suicide. Acts of great bravery resulting in certain death were no different in principle from jumping under a train. It may well be true that one form of suicide is stigmatized and the other is rewarded with a posthumous medal. But that is to see things through the layman's eyes, not the social scientist's. So: insufficient social integration can lead to self-destruction in the shape of egoistic suicide, while too much integration can have the same effect by way of altruistic suicide. Clearly, a delicate balance must be struck between the two tendencies if suicide is to be kept at bay.

The situation is further complicated by the addition of a third type—'anomic suicide'. This typically occurs under conditions of social upheaval, particularly those arising from economic crises. An industrial depression or a stock-market crash results in the dislocation of the humdrum pattern of daily life, thereby upsetting traditional values and expectations. A world turned upside-down is fertile ground for suicide. As Durkheim puts it, 'Every break in equilibrium . . . gives a boost to voluntary death.' (S 271)

Social equilibrium can be disturbed not only by economic misfortune, but by its very opposite. Those who come into sudden and unaccustomed wealth are thrown into as much moral confusion as those who become destitute. Both suffer from the effects of social 'de-classification', the up-ending of established hierarchies of esteeem and reward. Anomic suicide flourishes wherever there is a collapse of the rules and conventions which impose realistic limits upon expectations and desires. In the absence of such limits—the state of 'de-regulation'—wants are bound to escalate beyond the individual's capacity to satisfy them. Under these conditions of normlessness, people are as lost souls and life itself is stripped of any meaning.

The scourge of anomy does not, of course, affect everyone equally. Those most likely to be afflicted by it are people who work in commerce and industry, where anomy is in a 'chronic state'. Recently divorced men are also disproportionately affected, by virtue of the sudden loss of regulation and control upon the sexual passions. Durkheim tends to regard all forms of rapid social change as causes of disequilibrium, and therefore as pathological. That being so, the rate of anomic suicide served as a useful index of the health of society, a kind of social thermometer. Any sudden increase in the rate could be taken as a sign of collective sickness. Durkheim felt that modern society was in the throes of such a sickness because of its inability to halt the slide to anomy and to fill the normative vacuum with a morality suited to the times. His diagnosis of the ills of industrial capitalism comes as a rather surprising finale to a study seemingly devoted to a quite different and rather narrower topic. In both his diagnosis and his recommended cure for the malaise, Durkheim slips out of his white coat and assumes the role of political moralist. Such a transition was not something he would have felt defensive about. He always made it perfectly plain that the whole point of his scientific enterprise was to discover the best means of implementing rational social change. Sociology would forfeit its *raison d'être* if it ceased to be an instrument of human progress. Durkheim's critique of modern industrial society is considered in a later chapter. For the present, we keep to the study of suicide by examining the case levelled against it on procedural and substantive grounds.

III

As a practical application of the method elaborated in the *Rules*, the investigation of suicide is a qualified success. Durkheim most certainly does follow his own prescription to treat social collectivities rather than individuals as the object of enquiry. He explicitly disavows the relevance of personal motives for suicide and focuses instead upon those social realities that he called social facts—the constraints and pressures of collective life that impelled people to act in certain ways. He makes a powerful case for his contention that sociology has a domain of its own, distinct from those fields of endeavour which take individual behaviour as their datum. Many of the questions he succeeds in raising simply could not be answered within the confines of individual psychology. Again, as a demonstration of the uses of positivism it is a *tour de force*. It was the first time that statistical data had been assembled in such an imaginative way to test general propositions about society. There is nothing in the works of either Marx or Weber to match it. If Durkheim had never written another book before or after, *Suicide* would still have guaranteed his preeminence among the pioneers of the discipline.

All that being said, it is nevertheless the case that the treatment of the subject, and the method on which it rests, contain a number of serious flaws. Not least among these is Durkheim's equation of social facts with facts about the physical universe. Social facts, the counter-argument goes, do not possess the thing-like objectivity of facts about the natural world. The behaviour of people cannot be explained by methods similar to those used in understanding the motion of the planets. This is because, in the words of one critic, social facts 'are themselves constituted by the meanings attached to them by those agents whose acts, thoughts, and feelings they are, and ... such subjective interpretations are thus part of the reality to be "known"' (J 81). Social facts are, in other words, partially created by the reasons people give for their own behaviour. Laymen's ideas, far from being an obstruction to understanding, are of its very essence. The general view is summed up in Lukes's remark that Durkheim's method fails because 'the social scientist's data are not "hard data", his facts not "brute facts"' (Lu 12). Durkheim is declared guilty of ignoring the 'hermeneutic dimension'—the sociological approach which seeks understanding through 'the interpretation of the actors' world from within' (Lu 14–15).

Almost inevitably, Durkheim's positivistic stance is compared unfavourably with Weber's method of *Verstehen*—the attempt to explain an action by reference to the intersubjective meanings of the participants. Had Weber studied suicide, the implication seems to be, he would have produced a more rounded account by complementing the statistical data with interpretative material. It should, however, be remembered that Weber never in fact employed *Verstehen* in any of his enquiries. He was quite content to formulate general statements about capitalism, bureaucracy, the state, Protestantism, and the like, without feeling the need to enquire into the minds of capitalists, bureaucrats, state officials, and Protestants. Unlike Durkheim, Weber never followed his own rules. Marx was shrewd enough not to have set down rules of method, but his actual procedures were similar to those used by Durkheim and Weber. His analysis of class relations is couched in terms of the objective features of the capitalist system, a system driven by its own internal logic. There is no place in this scheme of things for the perceptions and feelings of workers or capitalists. If Durkheim is judged guilty in the high court of hermeneutics, he is in good company.

In choosing to study suicide along positivist lines, Durkheim was not unaware of the argument for motive. His rejection of it was based on a reasoned case; namely that it yielded very little in the way of explanatory fruit. There was a wealth of statistical material classifying suicides according to motive, but students of the subject 'had never in fact managed to derive a law of any interest' from such material (S 148). It is difficult to disagree with Durkheim on this point. What exactly would be the sociological pay-off from an examination of motive? Quite apart from the awkward fact that dead men tell no tales, a catalogue of motives, presumed or otherwise, does not add up to a theory. It certainly does not help to solve the problem raised by Durkheim—that is, why members of some social groups are more likely than others to kill themselves. Why, in other words, do social groups vary systematically in the propensity of their members to develop suicide motives?

This is not to say that motive is altogether irrelevant. It does have a part to play in the analysis, though not so much the motives of suicides themselves, as the motives attributed to them by others. Douglas has drawn attention to the importance of presumptive motive in the classification of death as suicide (Do 183–9). He suggested that the bureaucratic process involving police, doctors, and coroners' courts could affect the choice of verdict between suicide and accidental death. In many cases, the verdict could go either way, particularly if there were no witnesses to the event. Did the woman fall from the high window, or did she jump? Did the pop star mean to take an overdose, or did he simply misjudge? Did the soldier shoot himself intentionally, or did the gun go off while he was cleaning it? Questions of this kind do not always have a simple answer. In cases of serious doubt the coroners' courts take into account the personal circumstances of the deceased. Was there a history of depression or previous attempts at suicide? Was the deceased in trouble with the law? The courts, in other words, ask if there was a plausible reason or motive for suicide. If they decide that there was, the death is likely to be classified as suicide; if not, as accidental death.

The upshot of this is that the official statistics for suicide are a social construction based upon the perceptions, intuitions, and subjective judgements of fallible human agents. Seen from this angle, the statistics do not appear to be the kind of social facts that Durkheim regarded as 'things'. Given the way it is constructed, the suicide rate looks to be a very different thing from the rainfall rate.

Interestingly, Durkheim had considered this aspect of the problem, only to dismiss it. One of his reasons for disregarding the motives for suicide was that the official statistics of motive 'are in fact the statistics of the opinions about motive held by officials, often low-ranking officials' (S 144). Such people were not equipped to interpret and explain complex social facts. Their views about motive were therefore best ignored. Durkheim did not go on to question the ability of these same officials simply to record the fact of suicide. That was fairly unproblematic; errors were bound to be made from time to time, but these would be of a random nature and would not introduce any systematic bias into the figures.

This comfortable assumption has been challenged by Douglas and others following his lead. Douglas suggests that because of the stigma attaching to suicide, the recording officials are likely to come under subtle pressure from the deceased's family to bring in a verdict of accidental death. Such pressure could be more intense if insurance money is at stake, since claims are normally annulled if suicide is recorded on the death certificate. Douglas argues that family interventions of this kind are not random; groups are likely to vary in the amount of pressure their members will exert in the attempt to win a favourable verdict. Because suicide carries a greater social stigma among Catholics than Protestants, the former could be expected to press harder for a verdict of accidental death. That could explain why Catholics had a lower rate of recorded suicide than Protestants.

Douglas presents evidence from Swiss cantons which shows that the suicide rate in Catholic cantons is significantly lower than that in Protestant cantons, whereas the rate of accidental death is higher in the Catholic cantons. Are we to suppose that Swiss Catholics fall off the mountains more often than their Protestant neighbours, or is it more likely that Catholics take their own lives at about the same rate as Protestants but that their suicides are more often passed off as accidents? Durkheim's critics suggest that the second of these two possibilities is the more plausible, though there is no clear evidence to substantiate the case.

Differences in the suicide rate of religious groups are not the only bone of contention. The burden of Douglas's argument is that social groups in general vary in their wish to conceal suicide and in their capacity to exert pressure on relevant officials. Cohesive, tightly knit groups would be better able to achieve this end than isolated members of less integrated groups. Durkheim's key proposition that the rate of egoistic suicide varies in inverse ratio to the degree of group integration could thus be explained in these terms. People in close moral communities are just as vulnerable to the suicide current as everyone else; they are simply better able to persuade officials that suicides among their number were really accidental deaths.

The implication of this is that the official statistics for suicide are, in large part, a set of elaborate fictions. The true rate of suicide can never be known because the process by which it is recorded is open to systematic distortion. Durkheim's theory about the types and causes of suicide falls to the ground because the evidence on which it is based is badly contaminated. Contamination in one form or another affects not only the figures for suicide but virtually all official statistics. All social data that are formally processed are unavoidably impregnated with the moral ideas and assumptions of the classifying agents. To observe and analyse the process by which such data become socially constructed should be one of the prime tasks of sociology, a very different strategy from that which treats the data as 'hard facts'. It is thus not only Durkheim's method which is deemed to be fatally flawed but the entire positivist school.

Durkheim might well have had second thoughts about the validity of suicide figures had he considered at all carefully the manner of their compilation. But he need not have concluded that the figures as a whole were little more than fabrications or that the kind of distortions referred to above were sufficient to torpedo his theory. After all, he could have pointed out that the main counter-argument to his own was less than compelling. To propose, as his leading critic had, that social groups varied in their ability to affect the verdicts in coroners' courts is to advance a proposition about the unequal distribution of power and influence. Groups of greater influence are more successful in preventing suicide verdicts than groups of lesser influence. If this were in fact the case we should expect to find, among other things, that blacks in multiracial societies had a higher recorded suicide rate than whites, on the grounds that whites are able to exercise more pull than blacks. But figures for multiracial societies show that it is invariably whites who have the higher recorded rate. The suggestion that the lower rate for blacks in, say, the Deep South is due to their greater influence on local police, doctors, and court officials is difficult to take seriously.

Similarly with education. If the counter-theory were correct we should expect to find that the well-educated had a lower rate of recorded suicide than the uneducated; the families of the latter would generally be less well equipped for the subtle manœuvres required to steer the court towards a favourable verdict. And yet it is the educated who have the higher official rate. In many other cases of differential rates the theory lacks plausibility. The fact that men have a higher recorded rate than women, or that the widowed have a higher rate than the married, would seem to have little to do with differences in family pressure. What is more, no evidence has ever been presented to show that social groups actually mobilize themselves in this way to influence the courts, or that court officials are swayed by such attempts. In the light of all this, Durkheim could reasonably maintain that the official figures for suicide are sufficiently accurate reflections of reality to justify his use of them. Errors there would undoubtedly be, but not the kind of systematic distortions that would throw his theory into disarray.

To grant Durkheim the benefit of the doubt on this score would not thereby release him from the attention of his critics. His natural allies in the positivist camp have worries of their own about some of his procedures. It does not, for example, seem to be the best advertisement for the scientific method to support a theory of altruistic suicide with the aid of official statistics which recognize no such category. Durkheim has a way of juggling with the figures that enables him to confirm any proposition drawn from a hat. Creative accounting apart, certain of his working assumptions also give cause for concern—in particular his strategy of treating deviant cases as if they were the norm. Assuming it to be true that some groups are more suicide-prone than others, the fact remains that only a small minority within any such group will actually do away with themselves; the vast majority will soldier on through thick and thin. Yet Durkheim sometimes argues as if suicide were the rule rather than the exception, as may be illustrated by his explanation of suicide among the military. The evidence shows that the suicide rate among soldiers is invariably higher than that among young male civilians. In the period under review, the figures were 380 per million among the military, compared with 237 per million among civilian Frenchmen in the same age bracket. Durkheim's explanation for this difference is that 'the profession of arms gives rise to a moral constitution which draws a man powerfully to the act of self-destruction'. Because the military life 'is an extremely fertile ground for suicide, little is needed to actualize the tendency inherent in it; an example is enough. That is why it spreads like a trail of gunpowder among those predisposed to follow it.' (S 261).

Reading that, one could be forgiven for assuming that the figure of 380 soldiers per million referred to the hardy few who managed to resist the suicidal impulse, not those who succumbed to it. Durkheim is aware of the flaw in the kind of reasoning which uses deviant cases to explain general phenomena. He rejects racial characteristics as a cause of suicide precisely on these grounds. A racial group or type is a broad social category, 'suicide, on the other hand, is an exceptional event'. If race were a causal factor in suicide, we should expect the event to be much more general than it is. 'In a word, race cannot explain why out of a million people belonging to the same race, only 100 or 200 at the very most kill themselves each year.' (S 342) Quite. The question is why the same objection does not apply to each and every one of Durkheim's chosen categories.

Once it is acknowledged that in any social group, however suicide-prone, only a handful of people will take the fatal path, the focus of interest shifts to the few themselves. Framed in Durkheimian terms, do suicide victims in any given group have certain personal attributes in common which render them especially vulnerable? Some Protestants, some divorcees, and some soldiers are clearly at greater risk than others. Durkheim did not address himself to this question. Indeed, his rules of method precluded any such consideration. Not only were his chosen social facts, the suicide statistics, too crude an instrument with which to tackle the problem; his explicit disavowal of the relevance of individual psychology closed off any enquiry into it. He did grudgingly allow that differences in personal make-up were an element in the overall equation. In a brief, almost throwaway comment, he says that if in a given social group some people kill themselves while others do not, this is generally because 'the moral constitution of the former... offers less resistance to the suicide current' (S 366). It is the temperamentally least robust who are destined to meet the suicide quota. Ultimately, then, individual psychology is called upon to fill the explanatory gap left by positivist sociology.

Although this conclusion might not have been much to Durkheim's liking, he would not have seen it as a complete negation of his method. His aim was to account for the differential rates of suicide among various categories of the population, not to try and pinpoint the particular individuals at risk. Most propositions in the social sciences take a similar form to this; they are general statements about collective behaviour from which it is impermissible to draw conclusions about the conduct of any one person. The same holds true of the medical sciences: to demonstrate a close correlation between cigarette smoking and lung cancer tells us nothing certain about the life prospects of any one nicotine addict. As with suicide, there are other imponderables which upset the neat symmetry of our explanations. The fact that physiological studies shared certain problems with sociology would no doubt have confirmed Durkheim in his view of the scientific status of his discipline.

2 Law and order

I

In his tractate on method, Durkheim decreed that the pitfalls of subjectivism could best be avoided by the use of 'external' indices of the phenomenon under investigation. The elusive nature of social reality could only be apprehended by way of its measurable effects, some sociological equivalent of a thermometer. This, as we have seen, was the procedure he adopted in the explanation of suicide. But even before *Rules* or *Suicide* were published, he had followed the same precept in his analysis of social solidarity—the subject of his first major work, *The Division of Labour in Society* (1893).

In this, his doctoral dissertion, he sought to reveal the foundations of social order and expose the pathological elements that paved the way for turbulence and clamour. As always, the strategy was to show what a healthy organism looked like so that diseased versions could be more clearly recognized.

He opens his enquiry by declaring that the object under investigation—social solidarity—could only be apprehended by the aid of some external measure. Solidarity itself was not 'amenable to exact observation and especially not to measurement' (D 24). The most appropriate measure or 'visible symbol' was the law. 'Since law reproduces the main forms of social solidarity, we have only to classify the different types of law in order to be able to investigate which types of social solidarity correspond to them.' (D 28) This is a startling observation, particularly in view of the fact that Durkheim, for once, uses a key term—law—in its common-sense meaning. Law does not mean customary rules of behaviour, formal and informal; it means rules enforced by the threat of sanctions. In the case of advanced societies, it means statutes promulgated by the state. It is quite out of character for Durkheim to have posited a close connection between something so eminently social as solidarity and the administrative process of the central political power, a body whose impact upon society he is usually at pains to minimize. He himself appears to acknowledge this in responding to the kind of doubts that might have been raised by his own *alter ego*.

> It may certainly be objected that social relationships can be forged without necessarily taking on a legal form. [Some] . . . are regulated by custom. Thus law mirrors only a part of social life and consequently provides us with only incomplete data with which to resolve the problem. What is more, it is often the case that custom is out of step with the law. It is repeatedly stated that custom tempers the harshness of law, corrects the excesses that arise from its formal nature, and is even occasionally inspired with a very different ethos. Might then custom display other kinds of social solidarity than those expressed in positive law? (D 25)

The answer he gives to his own question is an unequivocal no. Law and custom are almost always in close harmony; indeed, custom is the very bedrock of law. The two are out of joint only in rare and exceptional cases. There might be some instances where solidarity rests upon custom alone, but these are 'assuredly of a very secondary order'. Because the 'law reproduces all those types that are essential . . . it is about these alone that we need to know' (D 26).

Durkheim distinguishes two general types of law, each defined according to the kind of sanctions that accompany them: 'repressive' and 'restitutive'. Repressive laws are those which punish the offender by inflicting injury upon him or causing him to suffer some loss or disadvantage. 'Their purpose is to do harm to him through his fortune, his honour, his life, his liberty, or to deprive him of some object whose possession he enjoys.' (D 29) Punishments imposed by penal law are the best example of repressive sanctions. They are always set by a specialized body such as a court of law or, in simple societies, a clan or tribal authority convened for that purpose. Restitutive laws, by contrast, do not bring down suffering on the head of the offender. Instead, they aim at 'restoring the previous state of affairs' (D 29). That is to say, they seek to re-establish the equilibrium that was disturbed by unlawful conduct. Civil law, commercial law, and administrative law are all examples of judicial rules which are backed by restitutive sanctions.

Repressive and restitutive laws correspond to two contrasting modes of social integration: 'mechanical solidarity' and 'organic solidarity'. Mechanical solidarity describes the condition of simple societies which have little in the way of specialized institutions. In such societies, lineage or kinship is likely to be the organizing principle behind most social activities. Individuals are barely conceived of as moral beings in their own right; they are but interchangeable units in the social whole. Under mechanical solidarity, normative consensus is virtually complete and 'every consciousness beats as one' (D 106). Durkheim dubs this type of solidarity 'mechanical' on the analogy with molecules in inanimate bodies, since these do not react on one another as do the molecules of living things. Mechanical solidarity rests upon the sameness of its constituent elements and therefore has a very limited capacity for internal change and development.

Organic solidarity is altogether different. In societies integrated along these lines, the parts that make up the whole are dissimilar from each other by virtue of the specific role that each plays in the division of labour. What binds them together is their inter-dependence. Being highly specialized, each can only perform in conjunction with all others, just as the various organs of the body can only function properly in unison. Under organic solidarity, the individual is not wholly submerged in the collectivity; everyone enjoys a measure of autonomy sufficient to allow the personality to develop along idiosyncratic lines, free of the 'yoke of the common consciousness' (D 118).

Durkheim suggests that the division of labour can only make headway at the expense of the common consciousness. There is a powerful tension between the individualizing impulse of the division of labour and the pressure for conformity exerted by the normative system. The evolutionary trend favours the division of labour, so that the consensual basis of society undergoes a marked alteration as the common consciousness loosens its monolithic grip. When every consciousness no longer 'beats as one', social integration has to depend more and more upon the imperatives of co-operative action. 'It is the division of labour that is increasingly fulfilling the role that once fell to the common consciousness. This is mainly what holds together social entities in the higher types of society.' (D 123)

This is the only occasion on which Durkheim even hinted at the possibility that society could be held together without the aid of normative bonds. In all his subsequent writings, the moral aspect of the problem is treated as paramount. Even in *The Division of Labour*, consensus is by no means reduced to a technical problem of social co-operation. The evolutionary drive towards greater differentiation certainly eroded the common consciousness spawned by mechanical solidarity; but in doing so it did not leave a moral vacuum in its wake. What happens is that the common consciousness becomes more general and abstract. Instead of laying down strict edicts for every aspect of behaviour it comes to embody broad moral precepts which leave a good deal of leeway for individual interpretation. People still feel their actions constrained by a moral force emanating from without, but this moral force is not as overpowering as that experienced under mechanical solidarity. Normative consensus under the advanced division of labour is therefore likely to be less than complete, enabling various kinds of deviance to flourish between the cracks.

Some forms of deviance would also occur under mechanical solidarity, notwithstanding the hegemonic power of the common consciousness. This was bound to happen because crime was an ineradicable feature of any society, however solidary it might be. In Durkheim's view this was no bad thing. Crime was a perfectly normal feature of any healthy society. Even among a society of saints, criminal acts would still be committed. Where the threshold of rightful conduct was raised to the highest level, the tiniest misdemeanour would provoke the same sense of outrage that serious felonies would call forth elsewhere. This highlights the fact that what counts as a crime does not inhere in the act itself, but in the kind of social reaction it arouses. An act may thus be defined as criminal when 'it offends the strong, well-defined states of the collective consciousness' (D 39). This should not be taken to mean that an act offends the common consciousness because it is criminal. Rather, 'it is criminal because it offends that consciousness. We do not condemn it because it is a crime, but it is a crime because we condemn it.' (D 40)

Crime is not simply a normal phenomenon, it is a salutary one; it is an 'integrative element in any healthy society' (R 98). Crime is in effect the other side of the coin of morality. Many of the

29

great moral reformers and innovators of the past were castigated as deviants by their contemporaries. Socrates and Christ died as criminals. The freedom of thought that we now take for granted could not have been won if the rules of conformity had not been infringed by adventurous spirits. Liberal philosophy itself was only made possible by the intellectual and moral courage of thinkers who were once branded as heretics. The criminal, then, was not a species to be despised; he played a useful and constructive part in social life. Crime, for its part, 'must no longer be considered as an evil which cannot be circumscribed closely enough. Far from there being cause for congratulation when it drops too noticeably below the normal level, this apparent progress assuredly coincides with, and is linked to, some social disturbance.' (R 102)

The fact that crime is perfectly normal, and even essential for the well-being of society, does not necessarily mean that we should applaud it. We do not rejoice in the experience of physical pain, but pain plays a vital part in the proper functioning of the body. Pain and crime both send out clear signals that something is wrong with the system and that remedial steps need to be taken. Durkheim draws no distinction between crimes of violence and breaches of the law on grounds of conscience or belief. His definition of crime precludes such a distinction; what counts as a crime is not the nature of the act itself, but the response of the community; and popular moral outrage can be just as fierce against heretics as against violent offenders. There is really no difference between Socrates and Jack the Ripper.

Deviants serve a socially useful role not only by pushing forward the frontiers of morality but also, somewhat paradoxically, by helping to define and clarify those same frontiers. This latter service is performed not so much by the criminal act itself as by the punishment that it calls forth. In the process of punishing the offender, the law which has been broken is publicly mended and reinforced. The moral sentiments flouted by the criminal are, by virtue of the punishment meted out, restored to their former equilibrium. Crime is thus functional because of the salubrious effect that its punishment has upon the law-abiding. Without it, people of upright conduct might soon fail to recognize the difference between right and wrong. Punishment, in fine, serves 'to maintain inviolate the cohesion of society by sustaining the common consciousness in all its vigour'. The absence of crime, and hence of punishment, 'would result in a relaxation in the bonds of social solidarity' (D 63).

Durkheim says that those who offend against the common consciousness deserve their punishment. They should be made to suffer for their crimes not because of any desire to inflict cruelty on the guilty for its own sake, but simply as a way of 'indicating that the sentiments of the collectivity are still unchanged, that the communion of minds sharing the same beliefs remains absolute, and in this way the injury that the crime has inflicted upon society is made good' (D 63). Punishment must therefore have a strong expiatory element, not because of the redemptive power of suffering, real or imagined, but because it is only through expiation that punishment can perform its integrative function. From a purely social point of view, punishment for its own sake is worthless.

II

Durkheim's analysis of crime and punishment is shot through with the evolutionary assumptions which came to inform all his subsequent works. As societies progressed along the path from mechanical solidarity to organic solidarity, so the nature of crime and punishment would also undergo change. Repressive law would gradually be replaced by restitutive law, and the more brutal forms of punishment would give way to more humane alternatives. This did not mean that repressive law was destined to disappear entirely. Rather, that as the division of labour became ever more complex, the balance between repressive and restitutive law would correspondingly shift in favour of the latter.

This proposition was not well received by social anthropologists, who were quick to point out that most tribal societies relied predominantly on the use of restitutive, not repressive, sanctions. One does not, in any case, have to be a social anthropologist to recognize the absurdity of the claim that the simpler the society, the harsher its forms of punishment. On this reckoning, the Australian aborigines—Durkheim's own candidate for the simplest known society—would rate as the most punitive of all, leagues ahead of any modern military dictatorship.

Durkheim himself evidently came to see that this proposition was untenable in its present form. Eight years after *The Division of Labour* he restated his argument in an essay entitled, 'Two Laws of Penal Evolution'. In this essay, he still maintains that punishment becomes less severe as societies become more advanced, but with one important proviso concerning the nature of the state. The revised proposition now reads: '*The intensity of punishment is the greater the more closely societies approximate to a less developed type—and the more the central power assumes an absolute character.*' (T 285)

It is the second of these two conditions which is the novel element. Very unusually for Durkheim, the state or central power is introduced as an agency capable of altering or disturbing the normal pattern of social evolution. The expected transition from repressive to restitutive law can be stalled or sent into reverse if the state takes on an absolutist form. Durkheim makes it clear that forms of state power vary independently of the degree of social complexity. Absolute rule is found among the simpler societies as well as the advanced. 'Nothing is less complex than the despotic government of a barbaric chief.' (D 166) Contrariwise, a modern state is not necessarily absolutist, be it ever so powerful. Absolutism is understood as a form of rule which brooks no resistance from other countervailing powers. As such, it can never be total; however despotic the regime, there will always remain some small corner of society beyond its reach. Nevertheless, there is a generic difference between absolutism and less centralized political systems, a difference which makes itself felt in the balance between repressive and restitutive law.

Durkheim's introduction of a political variable arose from his belated recognition that some of the most repressive regimes on record were well advanced on the road to modernity. European absolute monarchies were a case in point. In what was for him a rare excursion into history, he showed in grisly detail that crimes of lese-majesty reached their apogee in the seventeenth century, as did the severity of punishment meted out for such crimes. The administration of punishment was itself affected by the division of labour with the appointment of executioners and inquisitors, practised specialists in the manufacture of pain. As the absolute monarchies declined and gave way to more liberal, less centralized governments, so also did punishment become less and less barbaric.

Durkheim next poses the question of why punishment should be less cruel in societies that were more complex or less politically centralized. The answer lies in the changing nature of crime. True to his penchant for dichotomies, he proceeds to divide criminal acts into two basic types: those which are directed at collective things—such as offences against religion, state authorities, traditional practices, and the like; and those which cause injury only to the individual—homicide, robbery, rape, and so forth. Offences directed at collective things are designated 'religious criminality', by virtue of the fact that sacrilege and blasphemy of various kinds are the commonest offences in this category, as well as the fact that heads of state and venerable traditions are generally deemed to have a quasi-religious character. Crimes against individuals, on the other hand, are classified simply as 'human criminality' (T 300).

The two types of criminality differ profoundly because the collective sentiments that each offends, and the nature of the sanctions they provoke, are wholly unlike. In simple societies, the sentiments which are offended by criminal acts are collective in a double sense. They have collective things as their *object*, which is to say things that represent or symbolize the social over and above the individual. And they have collective things as their *subject*, in the sense that any hurt done to the common consciousness injures everyone in the community. In this situation, crimes are always experienced as offences against the whole society. Moreover, any offence against society is necessarily perceived as an assault upon the sacred objects and beings which personify society in the hearts and minds of its members. Religious criminality is therefore looked upon with the deepest abhorrence and punished with the utmost severity.

In advanced societies, by contrast, crime is not typically seen to be an assault upon the sacred realm. Human criminality has merely the individual as its object, and collective sentiments which pay homage to the sanctity of individuals do not have anything like the same force as those which are directed towards

33

the gods. There is all the difference in the world between attacking the deity and attacking the man next door. The latter offence need not be punished too harshly, because one man's injury does not threaten to shake the foundations of society. The social stakes are only really high where the common consciousness demands unswerving conformity to the rules. This cannot occur where the division of labour has worked its corrosive effect. As normative control grows ever more relaxed, crime is seen as a disturbance of the profane world merely, and so loses much of its capacity to send shock waves through society. As a consequence, punishment becomes progressively less savage.

This part of Durkheim's account is obviously a refined version of the thesis earlier set out in the *Division of Labour*. The original distinction between mechanical and organic solidarity has now been abandoned (never to reappear), as has the contrast between repressive and restitutive laws. But the general drift of the thesis is roughly similar; namely, that the punishment for crime tends to become more humane as societies make progress along the simple-to-complex continuum. The question still be addressed is why this evolutionary trend is disrupted by the intervention of political despotisms. Why should punishment be excessively harsh in societies with absolute rulers, even though such societies may be advanced in other ways?

Durkheim's answer is that wherever political power is absolute, breaches of the law are always treated as 'religious criminality'. The reason for this is that in such regimes the ruling despot almost always enjoys the status of a divine being. Consequently, offences against him or his office are looked upon as acts of sacrilege and punished with all the ferocity that religious crimes everywhere call forth. It is, of course, true that offences in absolutist regimes are not always directed against the despot or members of his entourage. Many, perhaps most, crimes are committed by the humble against their own kind. Nevertheless, such crimes are generally treated as if they were acts of lese-majesty. This is because the laws of the land 'are supposed to emanate from the sovereign and express his will, so the principal violations of the law appear to be directed against him' (T 305). Virtually any offence that disturbs the peace imposed by despotism is felt to be a religious crime and punished accordingly.

This proposition holds whether the despot is a shaggy tribal chief or a well-bred monarch. (Or, Durkheim's ghost might add, a megalomaniac ruler in a totalitarian regime.) Wherever power is monopolized in a single pair of hands, punishment will employ all the refinements of cruelty that the level of technology permits. Conversely, where power is diffuse or fragmented, be it in a tribal society or a modern state, there can be no equivalent crime of lese-majesty. As a result, punitive sanctions will be comparatively mild.

Durkheim makes it plain that the two factors explaining the nature of punishment vary independently. The impulses set in train by the passage from simple to complex are separate and distinct from those governed by the distribution of power. Given the independence of the two variables it should logically follow that the severity or otherwise of punishment would be a function of their combination. That is to say, on Durkheim's reasoning, the severity of punishment should reach its peak in societies which are both simple and absolutist, since in these societies criminality is religious on both counts. Likewise, punishment should be least harsh of all in societies which combine complexity with the diffusion of power. Durkheim could in other words have taken his analysis a stage further by seeking to show that the evolution of punishment was a cumulative effect of the two variables he had identified. But perhaps this would have been asking too much of a mind so attuned to slicing up reality into neat dichotomies.

A further difficulty is that he did not consider the two variables to bear equal explanatory weight. Consistent with his usual dim view of political agency, he held that the level of social development was the more decisive factor and that the form of state power was of secondary importance (T 299). In fact, a better case could be made for the reverse proposition. Durkheim did not of course live to see the arrival of full-blooded totalitarian regimes. Had he done so, he might have revised his view that monopolistic power was of lesser importance in explaining the dreadfulness of punishment. Even modern military dictatorships, which are usually less than absolute, have at their disposal a battery of sophisticated torments that no simple society could match. At the same time, Durkheim would probably have felt that such regimes confirmed his thesis concerning religious criminality. Dictatorships do appear to treat crimes against the state as if they were acts of sacrilege; challenges to the despot or his ruling clique often are seen as something akin to lese-majesty and punished accordingly. It would, though, sound like an exercise in Newspeak to claim that such punishment serves to reinvigorate the moral tone, rather than cow the rest of the population into submission.

III

In the essay on penal evolution, Durkheim puts forward another law, this time concerning the role of imprisonment. This states that: *'Deprivations of liberty, and of liberty alone, varying in time according to the seriousness of the crime, tend to become more and more the normal means of social control.'* (T 294) The general thrust of the argument is that the social practice of imprisonment passes through three distinct phases. Originally, prisons are places of temporary detention; then they become places for the administration of physical punishment; and finally, they become places of long-term detention, when incarceration in and of itself is the standard punishment.

Durkheim draws attention to the fact that imprisonment does not occur in the simpler societies. This is because in these societies responsibility is collective. It is not just the wrongdoer who is deemed guilty but the entire clan or kinship group. Under these conditions, it is unnecessary to hold the offender in detention since if he absconds others remain who can be punished in his place. Where, in any case, could an errant Nuer or Trobriander flee to?

Imprisonment only answers a social need when criminal responsibility is individual rather than collective. But even then the earliest prisons were not used as places of punishment, only as places of pre-trial detention. With the passage of time, however, the purpose of imprisonment underwent profound changes. First, prisons came to be centres of repressive punishment, institutions where offenders could be subjected to physical torment in a systematic fashion. The dungeons of the absolutist monarchs of the seventeenth and eighteenth centuries are the prime examples of this type of prison. Following the demise of these regimes, and their replacement by more liberal states, imprisonment came to signify something different from the administration of cruelty. Loss of liberty was regarded as a sufficient punishment in itself, so paving the way for a gradual amelioration of prison conditions. In a sense, prisons were needed in order that punishment could be made less violent. Once deprivation of liberty became accepted as a sanction in its own right, more barbarous punishments could be dispensed with. If locking offenders away had not been available as an option, how could penal law have evolved along more humane lines?

It might seem from this account as if the social need for prisons was sufficient to bring them into being. Interestingly, however, Durkheim pours cold water on this idea. In a departure from his usual functional stance he declares that, 'To explain an institution, it is not enough to establish that when it appeared it served some useful end; for just because it was desirable it does not follow that it was possible . . . However strong a need may be, it cannot create *ex nihilo* the means for its own satisfaction.' (T 297) Prisons, like all other institutions, came into existence only when there was both a need for them and when the social and material pre-conditions were in place. In the case of prisons, society had first to have attained a certain level of class or status stratification; at the very least there had to be a clear 'line of demarcation which . . . separates the holders of power from the mass of their subordinates' (T 297). When the power structure is such that the hovels of the poor are overshadowed by the ramparts and high walls of their masters' dwellings, the social conditions are ripe for prisons to make their appearance. Durkheim says that this is why the earliest prisons tend to be towers, dungeons, and the like—mere appendages to the castles, palaces, fortresses, and other buildings occupied by the high and mighty. A class structure, however rudimentary, was thus a prerequisite for the emergence of the prison.

This is about the only occasion on which Durkheim discusses crime and punishment in the context of power and social stratification. It is a pity that he did not pursue this line of enquiry further by asking whether law itself might be imbued with a class content. His bold assertion that 'law reproduces the main forms of social solidarity' forecloses any investigation into the possibility that legal rules could serve the interests of

37

a privileged stratum rather than the whole community. To promulgate laws and punish those who break them calls for the exercise of power, a political resource which is notoriously open to abuse. Even in the discussion of absolutism no questions are asked about the moral validity of the despot's laws; the focus is exclusively upon the nature of the sanctions which result from infractions of the law. In short, no attention is paid to the crucial matter of legitimacy.

It is as if Durkheim considered all regimes and legal systems to be legitimate by the very fact of their existence. Provided they enjoyed stability over a goodly measure of time, there could be no doubting their moral credentials. This would certainly be consistent with his general view that long-established institutions can never be 'false'. Institutions cannot be imposed upon a people artificially, either by force or by some act of political legerdemain. All are true, 'in their own fashion'. Take caste and class institutions as a case in point. These could never 'have become established and been maintained by artifice and ruse. They necessarily resulted from conditions of communal life. Societies have existed in which such inequalities were completely justified and had their *raisons d'être.'* (P 71) Even feudalism in its heyday was a just and rational system in so far as it was rooted in the immutable conditions of its time.

If settled regimes are always legitimate, the laws they uphold cannot systematically grate against common conceptions of natural justice. That is why Durkheim is keen to insist that wide discrepancies between law and custom will occur only in exceptional or 'pathological' cases. His leading proposition that law is the formal expression of social solidarity would collapse if legal rules were seen to be out of joint with popular or customary notions of justice.

Durkheim would undoubtedly have been aware of the Marxist or socialist theory of law as an instrument of domination by the bourgeois state. But he would have given little credence to a theory which presented the state as an organized conspiracy against the people. His own view of the state could hardly have been more different. He conceived of the modern state as an institution functionally equivalent to the human brain. The main purpose of the state was to 'think' on behalf of the community. It was well equipped to play this role by virtue of being endowed with a higher rationality than that available to the common consciousness. The fact that the officers of the state were flesh-and-blood creatures with interests and passions of their own did not suggest to Durkheim that they might use their powers to feather their own nest. He was quite aware that the state could, because of its unique authority, win a degree of autonomy from its social base. But it did not follow from this that a gulf would open up between the interests and sentiments of the common people and those of a political élite. Although it was true to say that 'the feelings of the collectivity are no longer expressed save through certain intermediaries', this did not imply that 'these feelings are no longer of a collective nature just because they are restricted to the consciousness of a limited number of people'. It is simply that 'certain personages or classes in society' happen to be especially well qualified to act as 'interpreters of its collective sentiments' (D 36–7).

In Durkheimian theory it is rather as if the common conscious-ness is too important to be entrusted to the ordinary people and has to be delegated to the 'brain' of society; just as in Leninist theory the only safe place for proletarian consciousness is in the enlightened mind of the vanguard party.

Durkheim's treatment of law and its relation to the state would have benefited from a stiff injection of Weber. Weber's concept of bureaucracy, in particular, would have served as a useful corrective to the bland assumption that the state and its incumbents were simply faithful servants to the common interest. Weber recognized that legal rules were the outcome of power struggles between conflicting parties and that victory did not necessarily go to those who had the best interests of society at heart.

The oddity is that Durkheim sometimes recognized this too, though he did not state it in quite such stark terms. Book III of the *Division of Labour* reads in part like a polemic against the social injustices springing from an outmoded and immoral distributive system. In these chapters, Durkheim abandons his air of scientific detachment and openly deprecates certain features of modern society, such as the inheritance of private property, the unfairness of labour contracts, the 'forced' division of labour, and untrammelled market competition. In deploring such practices

39

he was, by implication at least, casting doubt upon the moral validity of the laws in which they were enshrined. Such laws were decidedly not manifestations of the common consciousness or expressions of social solidarity. Quite the opposite; they undermined solidarity by flying in the face of natural justice and spreading the fatal social malaise of anomy. The full diagnosis of this malaise, and Durkheim's remedy for it, is the subject-matter of Chapter 4.

3 The social meaning of religion

Durkheim's theory of religion is more usefully thought of as a number of different theories which overlap at various points. He gives the attentive reader good value by offering separate accounts of the essence of religion, the origins of religion, and the social function of religion, as well as a general theory of knowledge of which religion is a special case. An examination of each of these theories is as good a way as any of getting to grips with what is rightly considered to be his most ambitious and startling work. Anyone who, on a first reading of the *Elementary Forms of the Religious Life*, fails to register any intellectual *frisson* must be made of very stern stuff.

Durkheim's quest for the essence of religion, the universal and irreducible substance common to all religious systems, is pursued in a manner fully consistent with his usual methodological stance. He was, as we have seen, prone to think of social reality as a world of deceptive appearances, a series of veils that had to be drawn aside by a practised hand to reveal the real matter beneath. Religion was a more deceptive phenomenon than most because it touched upon the very meaning of existence, of life and death itself. The highly charged relationship between people and their gods really was something much more than it seemed to be.

In order to lay bare the true essence of religion, Durkheim chose to make a microscopic examination of the simplest known system, the totemism of the Australian aborigines. This strategy followed from the application of a basic principle of his sociological method. 'Every time that we set out to explain something human taken at a given point in time—be it a religious belief, a moral rule, a legal principle . . . or an economic system—we have to begin by going back to its simplest and most primitive form . . . and then see how it gradually developed, grew more complex and evolved into what it became at the period in question.' (F 4–5) This is the very opposite procedure to that recommended by Marx. According to him, 'The anatomy of the human being is the key to the anatomy of the ape', implying that simple, less evolved forms could only be made intelligible in the light of forms at a more advanced stage (Ma 39). Feudalism only made sense against the backdrop of capitalism. On this reckoning, Durkheim should have launched his enquiry with an analysis of Christianity or Islam in order to penetrate the mysteries of totemism.

Leaving aside the question of whether Marx's method would in fact have delivered the goods, it may still be asked whether Durkheim's alternative was best suited to his declared aims. If the object of the exercise was, among other things, to discover the essence of religion, its defining characteristic, a comparative study might have seemed the more obvious choice. By examining a variety of religions, of differing levels of complexity, it would have been possible to isolate the core elements they shared in common. Durkheim appears to have contemplated this option only to reject it on the grounds that the major world religions were too highly evolved to yield their secrets. They had become too encrusted with bureaucracy and too immersed in theological argumentation, making it impossible to see the religious wood for the institutional trees. Totemism, by contrast, was uncluttered by all this paraphernalia; it was religion pared down to its bare essentials. As such it provided an accessible microcosm of all the great faiths. Understand totemism and you have understood them all.

Methodological doubts aside, this was not a position guaranteed to win Durkheim many friends among the churchly. The French Catholic community in particular would have regarded it as verging on the blasphemous to suggest that the beliefs and rituals of the mother Church were comparable to, and possibly derived from, the squalid superstitions of a bunch of painted savages. Even to hint at some evolutionary link between the holy mass and witchetty-grub ceremonies would have confirmed in many minds their long-held view that the Professor in the Sorbonne was, like his new pseudo-science, demonically inspired.

Atheists and anticlericals would have been equally offended, if for different reasons. They would have felt distaste for Durkheim's elevated regard for the religious life and for his insistence that there was nothing false or illusory about it. He held that religion expressed a profound truth which was beyond the grasp of the rationalist sceptic. Worse still from the latter's point of view, religion was the fount of almost every institution known to civilized society. Law, morality, contract, property, the arts, and even science, grew from religious beginnings. About the only important thing that was not unquestionably of religious origin was economic activity; concerning that, Durkheim was content to reserve judgement.

Hand-in-hand with this religio-centrism went a kind of piety towards the subject-matter of belief. Durkheim maintained that no account of religion could be adequate if it took an irreligious standpoint. Any such interpretation would necessarily be one which 'denied the phenomenon it was trying to explain' (Du 185). The suggestion was not merely that the sociologist should refrain from adopting an iconoclastic or even agnostic stance towards the study of faith; something more positive was called for. The investigator should seek to attain a state of mind similar to that of the worshipper. 'He who does not bring to the study of religion a sort of religious sentiment cannot speak about it. He is like a blind man trying to talk about colour.' (Du 184) Durkheim the unbeliever evidently felt able to make the required cognitive leap, just as the 'religiously unmusical' Weber was confident of his ability to penetrate the Calvinist mind.

In Durkheim's case, at least, the mental gymnastics would not have been too demanding, given the fact that what he understood by religion was very different from what it meant to actual believers. Religion was certainly not to be equated with a belief in the deity or the supernatural. Not all religions recognized gods or supernatural forces, so neither of these could qualify as an essential feature of religion. In any case, the elusive essence was unlikely to be anything so obvious or commonplace such as might suggest itself to the ordinary believer. Respect for the authenticity of religion was one thing; respect for the superficial notions of the dreaded layman was quite another.

In his usual manner, Durkheim prepares the ground for his own definition by bulldozing his way through all competing definitions. When the rubble of 'animism' and 'naturism' has been cleared away he sets up his own alternative: the distinguishing hallmark of all religious phenomena is that they 'always assume a bipartite division of the universe ... into two classes which comprise everything that exists, but which totally exclude each other' (F 56). These two mutually exclusive realms are the sacred and the profane. This division of the moral universe is the most fundamental aspect of all religions, from the most rudimentary to the most ornate. Indeed, in the 'entire history of human thought there is no other example of two categories of things so profoundly differentiated or so wholly opposed to each other' (F 53). To be sure, certain other moral dichotomies have exercised their sway over the common consciousness: good and evil, life and death, mind and body, heaven and hell, among others. But none of these has either the universality or the emotive power of the mutual opposition between sacred and profane.

Durkheim's notion of what constitutes the realms of sacred and profane does not, of course, correspond to anything known to theology. In his understanding, the sacred comprises 'things set apart and forbidden' (F 65). That is to say, sacred things are objects invested with powers so awesome that they inspire a sense of moral danger in those who come in contact with them. The realm of the sacred is a social minefield that must be negotiated with extreme caution and only along prescribed ritual pathways. Durkheim is emphatic that the sacred is not to be confounded with the holy and the good. Wicked and evil things are also part of the sacred because they too are 'things set apart and forbidden'. They too inspire awe, if only in the shape of revulsion and terror. In Durkheim's moral topography, God and the devil are close neighbours. More correctly, the two stand at opposite ends of the same sacred territory, the holy and the evil both opposing and complementing each other. The good 'needs' the bad in order to throw its goodness into high relief. 'Thus all religious life gravitates around two opposite poles between which there is the same opposition as between the pure and the impure, the holy and the sacrilegious, the divine and the demonic.' (F 586)

Although the two contrary poles within the sacred are in a state of continuous tension with one another, they are also united in their opposition to the profane. Durkheim does not offer a crisp definition of the profane, but what he means by it is the mundane workaday world, the sphere in which people go about their unremarkable, routine business. Profane is not to be equated with the blasphemous or sacrilegious of ordinary language, since these are aspects of the sacred. In effect, the profane is a residual category, a conceptual holdall for everything that cannot be fitted into the sacred. Profane things are simply those things which are *not* 'set apart and forbidden'.

The chasm between sacred and profane runs deep and wide, but there must nevertheless be a means of bridging it. A few dedicated souls may choose to live out their lives wholly within the confines of the sacred, never setting foot in the profane world. But society cannot be made up exclusively of monks and ascetics; most people have to spend most of their time in profane activities, with only occasional excursions into the sacred. Provision must therefore be made for a flow of social traffic between the two domains. Durkheim says that the manner in which this passage from one domain to the other is undertaken reveals the full extent of their opposition. In crossing the moral boundary, the individual undergoes what amounts to a symbolic process of death and rebirth. Most *rites de passage* which accompany vital stages in the life-cycle enact the symbolic death and resurrection of the initiates. Such rites are to be understood as a means of safe passage, as it were, between the sacred and profane spheres. Durkheim takes these rites to be a vivid testament to the duality of the two spheres that he has identified as the essence of religion. If the sacred world were not utterly unlike and opposed to the profane world, there would be no need for such elaborate ritual precautions in passing from one to the other.

The essence of the religious life is further clarified by a comparison with magic. Magic too is made up of beliefs and rites, myths and dogmas. Moreover, the forces which the sorcerer draws upon and the spirits he invokes are very often the same as those that religion brings into play. Much of the appeal of magic lies, in fact, in its debasement of holy things, as in the performance of the black mass. Nevertheless there is a great difference between magic and religion, an antithesis which earlier writers had remarked upon, Frazer in particular. Frazer had argued that magic was akin to science in its belief in the order and uniformity of nature. The sorcerer, like the scientist, sought to manipulate the natural world by the application of physical laws. Neither had any need to petition the services of a higher power because the desired result could be guaranteed by the correct use of technical procedures. Religion, on the other hand, appeals to a force beyond nature to achieve results; trust in God arises from the *failure* of magic to live up to its billing. Religion thus makes its appearance after magic, and probably evolves from it, a theory which Frazer held in common with Hegel (Fr 220–43).

Durkheim's distinction between magic and religion takes an altogether different tack. Predictably, his attention is drawn not to differences in practice, but to differences in social organization. Religion is always associated with a cohesive social group; it is invariably a 'Church', which is to say a community of believers. A Church in the Durkheimian sense need have no formal bureaucratic structure or priestly apparatus. Cults and sects also qualify as Churches, provided only that their members constitute a social collectivity. Magic, on the other hand, has no such social base. However numerous its adherents, they do not typically enter into relations with one another and so do not coalesce into a moral community. The relation between a sorcerer and his followers is similar to that between a doctor and his patients; each has a clientele, not a Church. 'There is no Church of magic.' (F 61)

II

The special character of the Church is spelled out more fully in the analysis of totemism, an ethnographic reconstruction designed to uncover the hidden function or purpose of religion. In Durkheim's rendition, totemism is a religious system based upon the clan, a sub-unit of the tribe. Clan members are not related by descent, but none the less they regard themselves as a single kinship group by virtue of the fact that they share the same name. This name is nearly always that of some natural species or other, usually an animal or a plant. This is the clan totem. Durkheim likens the totem to a badge or family coat of arms; it is an emblem engraved or painted on some physical object as a symbolic representation of the group. The totem is not simply the name and emblem of the clan, it is also of the deepest religious significance. 'It is the archetypal sacred thing.' (F 167)

In their religious ceremonies, Australian tribes place great importance on the use of certain artefacts called *churinga*, which are bits of polished stone or wood engraved with the clan totem.

46

These objects are not themselves in any way remarkable. What translates them from profane things into sacred things is the totemic sign emblazoned on them. That is to say, the 'images of the totem have a greater potency than the totem itself' (F 189).

Durkheim wonders aloud why the emblem or symbolic representation of the clan should be invested with such extraordinary significance. His answer is, because the concept of the clan is too abstract and remote to be grasped in all its complexity by the primitive mind. Even among civilized peoples, symbols are frequently used to represent ideas and sentiments. And these symbols then tend to become the object of popular emotion; think of the national flag or the crucifix. If sophisticated minds work in this way, small wonder that more rudimentary intelligences should elevate the symbol above the thing being symbolized.

Durkheim recounts in painstaking detail the manner in which various clans pay homage to their totems. But beneath the ethnographic exotica a question is slowly taking shape: when these people worship their totemic emblems what are they *really* doing? Members of the kangaroo clan certainly appear to be in close spiritual communion with this creature whose name they have adopted and with whom they declare a natural affinity. But surely they cannot actually be worshipping an animal? Surely there must be more to it than meets the eye?

Durkheim assures us that there is. He says that when members of the clan unite in religious celebration of their totem, what they are in fact worshipping, unbeknown to themselves, is the clan itself. Religious sentiment is a social force generated by the clan and directed towards an object which is the figurative embodiment of the group. This holds true not just for totemism but, by extension, for every religion, even the most advanced. What the believer experiences as an intimate relationship between self and god is in reality a collective force manufactured by society for the benefit of society. Religion is thus to be understood as 'a system of ideas by means of which people represent to themselves the society of which they are members and the opaque but intimate relations they have with it. This is its essential function.' (F 323)

The implication is that without religion and its symbolism, society would lack a proper consciousness of itself. Worship is the means by which a community celebrates its own identity and through which the bonds of social life are invigorated and renewed. This is what religion is *for*, even though the devout may be blissfully unaware of it. It is because religion performs this vital service for society that it has everywhere passed the acid test of time, despite the manifold errors it has proclaimed as truths. The fact that religious beliefs are often empirically false does nothing to undermine the faith because such beliefs are merely secondary aspects of religion. Its principal purpose is unimpaired because this has little or nothing to do with the scientific validity of its claims. Because religion succeeds in its paramount function, which is to cement society into a moral community, it can commit as many errors as it pleases without falling into discredit. However wrong it may be, no religion can be 'false', for the simple reason that it expresses something absolutely genuine—the spirit or consciousness of the community. A society without religion would suffer from acute normative impoverishment, with potentially fatal consequences for solidarity and order.

The functional interpretation of religion received a rather warmer reception among anthropologists than among sociologists, even though some of the former were characteristically snooty about Durkheim's ethnographic competence. It did seem to make good sense to see religion in small-scale societies as a force for moral cohesion. Under conditions of mechanical solidarity there was but a single Church, a moral system to which practically everyone subscribed. Advanced societies based on organic solidarity were a different matter. Among many or most of these, religion was less likely to be a unifying force than a divisive one. A functionalist theory of religion does not offer a promising framework for the study of societies split between Catholics and Protestants, Jews and Muslims, Hindus and Sikhs. A society with more than one Church is a society asking for trouble.

Durkheim might possibly have defended his functionalist position by declaring that a society with more than one Church was a contradiction in terms. He often comes close to saying that a society worthy of the name is, by definition, a single moral community, so ruling out by fiat the possibility of normative cleavage. This would seem to imply a tacit distinction between state and society; states could be divided internally along religious lines, whereas societies could not. A defence of the functionalist position along these lines would, however, have raised other difficulties, not least of all because Durkheim frequently refers to society when he means France the nation-state. The difficulty is one of his own making, and arises from his initial assumption that a complex religion, with its inbuilt capacity for igniting passion, is simply totemism writ large.

III

Durkheim was intent on explaining not only the essence and the function of religion, but also its social origins. In some respects this was the riskiest part of the whole enterprise. Even totemism, allegedly the most primitive of all religions, had been a going concern for millennia before it was captured for the record. Its origins were lost in the mists of time, accessible only through the lavishly embroidered recollections of myth and popular legend. This did not trouble Durkheim unduly since he saw the problem less as one of historiography than of sociological reasoning. The beginnings of the institution could be deduced from the existing social practices of the aborigines.

He takes as his starting-point the seasonal variations in the domestic economy of the tribe. Two distinct ecological phases were discernible, each corresponding to a particular set of activities. In one phase, the population is scattered and fragmented into independent family units, each busily occupied in hunting and gathering on its own behalf and having little or no commerce with other family groups. All activities in this phase are very much of the profane variety, humdrum and laborious, with almost nothing to break the monotony. In the second phase, all this changes. Now families of the clan are summoned together for a ceremonial extravaganza known as a corroboree. The 'moral density' arising from this gathering together generates a state of intense emotional excitement among the participants. The 'mere fact of social concentration acts as an exceptionally potent stimulant. Once they are assembled, their coming together gives off a kind of electricity which rapidly transports them to an extraordinary pitch of exaltation.' (F 308) Under these emotionally supercharged conditions, all normal rules of conduct and decorum

49

go by the board. Because the savage, even at the best of times, has only a precarious grip upon his passions, he quickly loses any vestige of self-control during the corroboree. Then he can be seen 'running amok like a madman, indulging in all sorts of reckless-ness, crying, shrieking, squirming around in the dust ... brandish-ing weapons in a threatening manner ...' and generally behaving like an England football supporter abroad. (F 308)

The 'effervescence' engendered by the social concentration of the clan causes its members to undergo a kind of metamorphosis. They become transformed, suddenly conscious of powerful forces at work within them of which they had previously been unaware. Nothing could be in greater contrast than their mental state during this phase of effervescence and their state of mind during the phase of routine economic activity. So arises an awareness of the polar opposites of sacred and profane, the two mutually ex-clusive moral realms which are the very essence of religion. 'It is thus amid these effervescent social milieux and from this efferve-scence itself that the idea of religion appears to be born.' (F 313) The origin of religion is to be found not simply in society, but society in a state of collective delirium.

Durkheim's portrayal of effervescent group behaviour has some similarity to contemporary theories of crowd psychology. The prominent social psychologist, Gustave Le Bon, was one of several writers who had characterized the conduct of the mob as a form of action in which the passions had been cut loose of all rational control. People did things as part of a mob that they would never dream of doing as individuals. The effervescence engendered by the mob or crowd led almost invariably to morally reprehensible behaviour. Durkheim's theory of religion marked a departure from this view by proposing that collective excitement could lead to a virtuous outcome. This is not to say that he gave his seal of approval to mob action. In his lectures on *Moral Education* (1925) he drew a clear distinction between the effervescence of the mob and that of a properly constituted social group.

> Collective action, according to the way its influence is used, may enhance the good or increase the evil. Should its influence be abnormal, then, precisely because it excites and intensifies individual energies, it drives them on the road to catastrophe

with all the greater energy. This accounts for immorality developing so readily in mobs and quite often reaching an exceptional degree of violence. The mob, we know, kills easily. A mob or crowd is a society, but one that is inchoate, unstable, without regularly organized discipline. (ME 150)

In other words, a mob is not a moral community; it has no Church. Effervescence produced from this tainted source is bound to be pathological, unlike that emanating from the clan or some other genuine social group. As always, it was the social make-up that was ultimately decisive.

In locating the origin of religion in collective behaviour, Durkheim necessarily plays down the role of outstanding individuals. Because religion emerges from the moral density of mass interaction there is no obvious place for a prophet or seer, the inspirational figure who articulates the faith or proclaims a new doctrine. In short, the charismatic leader is only a minor character in the drama. He is not altogether absent though. Durkheim does occasionally refer to 'prophets and founders of religion ... men whose religious consciousness is exceptionally sensitive' (F 324). He also gives a vivid description of a notional charismatic leader haranguing his followers. 'His language has a kind of grandiloquence that would sound ridiculous in ordinary circumstances; his gestures are somewhat overbearing, his very thought is impatient of moderation and easily slips into all sorts of extremism. It is because he feels within him an abnormal overabundance of forces which overflow and seek to burst beyond him ...' He is a man possessed by 'the demon of oratorical inspiration' (F 300). The social significance of the charismatic leader is, however, immediately devalued. He is not to be thought of as Weber's revolutionary firebrand, a prophet with a startling new message that will turn the world upside-down. He is merely the 'group incarnate and personified' (F 301). No one individual could be singled out as a creative force in what was a pre-eminently collective enterprise. The charismatic figure could only be a megaphone for amplifying the chorus of society.

Had Durkheim conceded a greater role to charisma he would have been obliged to take into account religious doctrine, something he was clearly loath to do. Doctrine is the life-blood of charisma, the stuff on which the prophet flourishes. A Christ, a Muhammad, a Luther mobilizes the faithful by excoriating the old dogmas and proclaiming a shockingly new set of principles. And, as Weber's sociology of religion demonstrated, variations in belief led to variations in behaviour: Catholics, Jews, and Protestants followed different courses of social action because they were driven by different religious motivations. Doctrine made all the difference in the world. Moreover, any complex doctrine was open to a variety of interpretations among the faithful, according to their class or status position. The concept of a single Church does not rest comfortably alongside the brute facts of social hierarchy.

Durkheim's response to this would probably have been that Weber's sociology of religion did not get to the root of the problem. A concern for the niceties of doctrine was bound to highlight the differences between religions, thereby distracting attention from what they shared in common. Such an approach could not hope to answer the really crucial questions of what religion actually was, how it was distinguished from the secular, and how and why it arose in the first place. Weber's analysis of the great world religions does not even raise, let alone solve, any of these sociological problems.

Durkheim would also have been unimpressed by Weber's claims for the explanatory importance of charisma. He would have said that prophets might prescribe and articulate a certain set of beliefs, but could not themselves create religious feeling and sentiment. A charismatic leader could only work upon and fashion such sentiment that was already in existence; he could not himself bring into being the raw material of religion. No one individual, however inspired, could possibly have originated anything so profound and universal as the distinction between sacred and profane. Such a division of the moral universe could only be a product of collective life and would have to arise prior to any particular religious doctrine. The religious consciousness could be thought of as a reservoir of sentiments which this or that prophet could draw upon and shape to his own design. A prophet is thus to religion what a fine poet is to language: someone who makes brilliant individual use of a socially constructed medium. But as far as the *origin* of religion is concerned, the charismatic leader is of small relevance. He would be but one more bubble in the collective effervescence.

Interestingly, Durkheim, unlike Weber, draws an implicit distinction between religious charisma and political charisma. Whereas the prophet is merely the group personified, the political leader can be an independent force and an instrument of radical change. In his discussion of despotism, he suggests that the earliest absolute rulers were the 'first individual personalities who have risen from the mass of society'. Because of their untrammelled powers, despotic chiefs could act as social innovators, impressing their will upon the collectivity and altering the course of its action. 'Dominating society, they are no longer constrained to follow its every movement. Doubtless it is from the group that they draw their strength. Yet once their strength is organized, it becomes autonomous and renders them capable of personal action. Thus a source for initiative is opened up which until then did not exist. Henceforth there is someone who can engender something new, and even depart from collective customs. The balance is upset.' (D 143)

Durkheim nowhere suggests that religious charismatics have a comparable ability to upset the balance by rising above the mass and imposing their individual will upon the collective consciousness. He no doubt felt that religion was a far more elemental and primordial activity than politics, and that the scope for individual innovation was therefore much more limited. At any rate, he did not indicate that there was anything in the sphere of political belief remotely similar to the dualism of sacred and profane. Nor did he ever propose that political ideology might have an integrative part to play in the maintenance of social solidarity. Religion was the thing that really mattered, and there was no call for a companion volume on the elementary forms of the political life.

IV

Durkheim's theory of religion is also a treatise in the sociology of knowledge. He declares that all known religions have been 'systems of ideas which tend to encompass the universality of things and to give us a complete representation of the world'

(F 200). In some respects, religion has been a kind of primitive sociology, a pre-Durkheimian sociology; it has provided even the simplest peoples with a framework for bringing conceptual order to the moral universe. Durkheim says that the logical categories used by primitive groups are closely bound up with their forms of social organization. That is to say, the classification of natural phenomena follows from the way that tribal life is arranged. Take, for example, the notion of hierarchy. The classification of nature often entails the ordering of things according to certain criteria of dominance and subordination. Nature is perceived in this way because social life is also governed by similar rules. People would 'never have thought of arranging their knowledge in this manner if they had not previously known what a hierarchy was' (F 211).

This argument had been set out more fully in his earlier essay on *Primitive Classification* (1903). One of his targets in that essay was Frazer, a favourite Aunt Sally. Frazer had claimed that the social relations between individuals were based upon the logical relationship between things. Clans were divided and subdivided in a particular way because material objects were classified along similar lines (P 82). Durkheim insisted that precisely the opposite was the case: forms of social organization reproduced themselves in the classification of things. The logical categories imposed upon the natural world were derived from the model of tribal formation. The Mount Gambier tribe, for example, is divided into ten clans, 'consequently, their entire world is divided into ten classes or families each with its own distinctive totem', and which, when taken in combination, 'constitute a complete and systematic representation of the world' (F 219).

Durkheim comes perilously close to positing a one-to-one relationship between social formations and types of cognition. But the lapse into outright social determinism is ultimately resisted, most notably in his comments upon the connection between the secular and sacred worlds. He accepted that religion was rooted in the material realities of social life, but wished to distance his own position from that of the Marxists. 'In showing religion to be something essentially social, we do not mean to say that it limits itself to translating into another language the material forms of society and its basic necessities.' (F 605) Religious ideas and sentiments have a life of their own, and are not mere epiphenomena of structural forces. 'There is a considerable distance between society as it is objectively and the sacred things which express it symbolically. The impressions actually felt by men, and which were the original basis of the construction, have had to be interpreted, embellished and transformed until they became unrecognizable.' (F 544–5) Once religious energies have been released by the intensity of social interaction, they are able to win for themselves a large measure of normative autonomy. Religion can then unfold under its own momentum and according to its own internal logic, far removed from the grubby concerns of material life. The possibility that religion in its rarefied state could represent anything as crude as class interests would seem fanciful in the extreme.

The most systematic form of knowledge was of course science. Durkheim was fairly unusual among the unbelievers of his day in seeing no conflict between scientific and religious modes of thought. There could, in his view, be no conflict for the simple reason that 'the fundamental notions of science are of religious origin' (F 616). Totemism, for example, was a religious system in which things were classified according to certain broad principles, which is one of the hallmarks of scientific procedure. Science and religion both seek to make reality intelligible with the aid of concepts; also, both attempt to point up the connection between things through the workings of cause and effect. Without the intellectual discipline of religious thought, the mind could not have become attuned to the rigours of scientific method.

A further reason why science and religion made comfortable bedfellows was that the scientific notion of truth originated from the same source as religious belief—the common consciousness. The idea of truth or scientific validity was initially a purely social construct. A fact was deemed to be true because the collectivity held it to be so. Science today demands rather stricter criteria of truth, but even so most things that we now take to be true are not scientifically validated; their truth depends largely on collective endorsement. For Durkheim there can be no such thing as a collective untruth, the reason being that if it 'were at variance with the nature of things it would not have been able to establish a far-reaching and continuous dominion over the mind' (F 625). Religion was the supreme example of this. It could only have become so deeply rooted in society because it expressed a fundamental truth.

This assumption that long-established social practices and institutions are necessarily right and proper is central to Durkheim's cast of thought. It is, for him, 'an essential postulate of sociology that a human institution cannot rest upon an error and a lie' (F 3)—an assertion which would be unlikely to cut much ice among, say, sociologists of slavery, let alone the slaves themselves. It is in any case a little eccentric to speak of institutions as being true or false, as though they were testable propositions. To confound matters even more, the notion of truth itself turns out to have a Durkheimian trademark. All religions, for example, are declared to be 'true in their own fashion' (F 3). Such a relaxed definition would confer the status of truth on almost anything: astrology, witchcraft, even monetarism.

Science and religion may not be at odds with one another, but their paths do diverge over time. Science gradually takes over the cognitive aspects of knowledge, leaving religion to cater to the special needs of the soul. In the beginning, religion saturated the whole of social life, 'everything social was religious—the two words were synonymous. Then gradually political, economic, and scientific functions broke free from the religious function, becoming separate entities and taking on more and more a markedly temporal character. God, if we may express it in such a way, from being at first present in every human relationship, has progressively withdrawn. He leaves the world to men and their quarrels.' (D 119)

The decline of religion could, presumably, make itself felt in two different, though not mutually exclusive, ways. The realm of the sacred could simply contract in relation to the profane, so that fewer and fewer things would be set apart and forbidden. Alternatively, the sacred could become less awesome than it formerly was. The divide between sacred and profane would still exist, but the gulf would be less deep and the passage from one to the other less fraught with moral danger. Whichever tendency Durkheim had in mind when speaking of God's withdrawal from the world, he did not subscribe to the view that religion was destined for oblivion. The survival of religion was guaranteed because it was an essential prop to society. It was not an optional extra.

However, the religion of the future would be very different from all previous varieties. The most spectacular break with the past consisted in the fact that the ultimate object of veneration would not be society as such, but the individual. Durkheim paints a picture of modern society as a place beset by the centrifugal forces of anomy. Stable communities have been eaten away by the corrosive acids of social and geographical mobility; people have turned in upon themselves and no one knows his neighbour. The only thing they now have in common is their humanity. 'This idea of the human person . . . is therefore the sole idea that survives, immutable and impersonal, above the changing tides of particular opinions . . . In consequence, there remains nothing that men may love and honour in common, apart from man himself. This is why man has become a god for man, and why he can no longer turn to other gods without being untrue to himself.' (I 26)

The new religion of individualism was not to be understood as a doctrine of personal licence. It offered no banquet for the self to gorge upon. Individualism, unlike egoism, was rooted in self-restraint and moral discipline. To act as individual was to subordinate personal interest to the common good. Individuals, unlike egoists, were products of society; they were, so to speak, society's representatives on earth. The religion of individualism may have deified the person, but only because that person is a surrogate for society. The contrast between the new religion and the old may therefore not be so great after all. The individual is simply the totem in a modern guise, the illusory focus of veneration whose real object is the collectivity.

Durkheim clearly assumed that the religion of individualism, what we would now think of as a doctrine of human rights, would be adequate to unify society. But a commitment to the rights of the individual would seem to be compatible with a variety of political ideologies. Conservatives, Liberals, and Social Democrats, among others, could all endorse the ideals of human rights and individual liberties while being seriously at odds over matters of social equality and distributive justice. The religion of individualism seems to harbour more than one Church, a Durkheimian recipe for disaster.

Durkheim might perhaps have felt that if individualism was accepted without question as the master doctrine of society, then political and social conflict over other issues would not seriously upset the moral equilibrium. The difficulty is that he never made clear whether certain types or degrees of dissension might be compatible with the notion of an orderly society. He never addressed the problem of how far a house could be divided without the walls falling in. He seems to have had a strong aversion to conflict of any kind, and most of his proposals for political and social reform are aimed at its elimination rather than its domestication. In his analysis of the relationship between state and civil society, on the other hand, he does concede that there is a permanent tension between these two spheres, a mutual opposition which is actually beneficial both to society and the individual. How conflict is to be resolved or avoided in the distribution of resources and political power is one of the principal themes of the following two chapters.

4 Capitalism, socialism, and distributive justice

As the preceding chapters will have made clear, the recurring theme in all Durkheim's writings is the problem of order. At whatever point on the exegetical compass he begins any enquiry it leads back inexorably to the question of what makes society possible. Durkheim seems to have been haunted by the thought that modern society in particular was a fragile affair, a potentially unstable mix of elements that was always on the verge of dissolving into chaos. The whole purpose of his sociology was to identify the sources of disequilibrium in order that remedial measures could be put in hand. He often stressed the urgency of this task, as though he saw himself in a race against time with the gathering forces of anarchy.

It must, however, be made plain that Durkheim's ideas have little affinity with that strand of conservative thought which extols the virtues of order at any price. He was never in any doubt that the only kind of order worth having, indeed the only kind that was viable, was one founded on principles of social justice. Notwithstanding his commitment to the ideal of normative consensus, he was under no illusions that such a consensus could be imposed upon a society disfigured by archaic inequalities. The good society, an orderly and cohesive moral community, presupposed a system of distributive justice that answered to the needs of the times.

Durkheim was acutely aware that such a system was lacking in his time and place. The flaws that he pointed to in the old order were many and deep-seated and called for more than cosmetic adjustment. Some of his strictures could be read as a critique of capitalism, though this was a term that he chose not to bandy about. He certainly never defined modern society as capitalist, believing perhaps that the mode of production was not its most salient feature; economic activity was the preserve of the profane world, far removed from the sacred core. In any case, once society had reached the stage of organic solidarity, variations in the mode of production would presumably be matters of small importance, just as for Weber the differences between capitalist and socialist production would be insignificant once society had reached its bureaucratic climax. But although Durkheim did not generally refer to capitalism by name, his arrows were directed at two targets which are almost synonymous with it: private property and the free market.

It was not the institution of private property as such which met with Durkheim's disapproval, but the rights of social inheritance. The transmission of wealth through the family line was profoundly unfair because it conferred upon people advantages which bore no relation to their personal merit or their services to society. Such an arrangement had wide repercussions, in that it 'invalidates the whole contractual system at its very roots' (L 237). Durkheim wanted to level the playing-field so that all contestants would have an equal chance of becoming property owners by dint of their own exertions. Because property inheritance was 'bound up with archaic concepts and practices that have no part in our present day ethics', the result was to give property itself a bad name (L 201).

This was unfortunate because the institution of private property was a perfectly normal phenomenon. Its origins were to be found in communal life, where it was invested with a sacred character. The evolutionary trend from communal to individual rights of ownership did not divest property altogether of its religious aura. As the individual became the ultimate object of religion, the sacredness of his property came to reflect this new circumstance. The individualization of property can thus be seen as part of that general development from mechanical to organic solidarity by which man emerges as a distinct moral entity from the shadow of the collectivity. The individual affirms himself as such by claiming exclusive rights to things; without the distinction between mine and thine, the identity of the person would be little more than a blur.

Significantly, Durkheim does not distinguish between property as personal possessions and property as a productive resource. The ownership of a hat, and of the firm that manufactured it, are accorded equal status. Since, on this reckoning, everyone is a proprietor of some sort, there can be no conflict of interest between a propertied and a propertyless class. While that does appear to be the logical conclusion to be drawn from the blanket definition of property as ownership, Durkheim does in fact acknowledge the existence of conflict between capital and labour. In his discussion of contractual relations, he makes the point repeatedly that contracts can only be considered just if the two parties meet on equal terms. Contracts between workers and their employers patently did not meet this condition.

> If one class in society is obliged, in order to live, to secure the acceptance by others of its services, whilst another class can do without them, because of the resources already at its disposal, resources that, however, are not necessarily the result of some social superiority, the latter group can lord it over the former. In other words, there can be no rich and poor by birth without there being unjust contracts. (D 319)

Durkheim does not explain how parties to the labour contract are to be placed on a more equal footing while one of them enjoys the power conferred by capital ownership. One obvious way of correcting the balance, in part at least, would be to enhance the power of labour by encouraging trade unions. But this solution would not have appealed to Durkheim, given his view of trade unionism as a 'retrograde' movement which 'runs counter to our general direction in historical evolution' (G 146–7). In any case, the power of capital did not necessarily give its owners an unfair advantage. As the above statement about just contracts indicates, the balance is only upset if the ownership class has resources which are undeserved. Where capital is justly acquired and responsibly used, the power flowing from it is legitimate. This, however, was rarely the case, with the consequence that the present relations between the two sides of industry were more akin to a state of civil war than to the civilized behaviour of genuine contracting parties.

The fact that Durkheim's objection to property was confined to the rules of its inheritance should not be taken to mean that his commitment to social equality was lukewarm. After all, the inheritance of wealth through the kinship line is the very corner-stone of class stratification. The laws of inheritance ensure that family dynasties can be preserved intact down the generations, providing the long-term continuity which fosters class identity and class culture. Without property inheritance to guarantee the reproduction of social privilege from fathers to sons, mere social inequalities would not readily crystallize into a stratified order. Durkheim's opposition to inheritance thus struck at the very heart of the class system.

His critique of the free market was also made on grounds of unjust deserts. A distributive system based upon the laws of supply and demand was blind to the need to link the level of reward to differences in merit and social worth. It was deeply offensive to popular conceptions of distributive justice to allocate benefits according to the degree of bargaining strength or in the manner of a public lottery. Durkheim held that in every society, in any given period, there was a widely accepted set of beliefs and expectations pertaining to the level of reward that was thought appropriate to the various occupational groups. This informal system was continuously evolving in line with changes in the division of labour and the wealth of society. But its purpose was always the same— to specify 'the maximum degree of affluence to which each social class may legitimately aspire' (S 126). An occupational group could not exceed its notional quantum of affluence without upsetting popular sentiment and, by implication, bringing the entire distributive system into disrepute. That was exactly the effect that the market was having.

It was not simply that market forces were amoral; they were subversive of the self-restraint essential to an orderly society. Durkheim's anguish about the false needs spawned by the market anticipates by several decades the diatribes of the Frankfurt School. He bemoaned the fact that modern society was in the grip of the 'dogma of materialism' and that production instead of being treated as a means to an end 'has become the highest aim of individuals and societies'. The result was that people's appetites had been whetted beyond the point at which they could be satiated. This 'eruption of desires has been intensified by the ... almost infinite extension of the market ... From top to bottom of the social ladder greed is aroused which can find no satisfaction. There is a thirst for novelties, unfamiliar delights, vague sensations, which lose all their savour as soon as they are tasted.' (S 284–5) Marcuse could hardly have put it better. One of the worst sins in Durkheim's book was to heighten people's expectations above the level at which they could reasonably be met. To open up a gulf between desires and the means for fulfilling them would lead to frustration and resentment, potent sources of clamour and disturbance. The competitive instincts unleashed by the market and its inbuilt drive to raise the threshold of wants made it too explosive to contain within an orderly social framework. 'The anarchy of the market-place' is one of those Marxist terms that Durkheim might have felt tempted to use, had it not come from such a tainted source.

To find the existing pattern of inequality morally offensive is not necessarily of course to be out of sympathy with the very idea of inequality. Durkheim was firmly within that liberal tradition which holds that certain inequalities are not merely compatible with social justice but essential to it. Inequalities, to be just, had to rest upon rational principles, not upon convention or tradition. His views on this score were set out in his discussion of 'abnormal' forms of the division of labour, more especially that abnormal form known as the 'forced' division of labour. The division of labour was forced, rather than normal or spontaneous, if there was a serious mismatch between the functional importance of positions and the abilities of their incumbents. This was all too frequently the case; positions vital to the well-being of society were often staffed by mediocrities and dullards while truly gifted people were forced to squander their talents performing routine tasks. This was both a waste of society's human resources and an affront to justice. Durkheim was an early proponent of meritocracy in wishing not only to allocate talent more rationally but also to shower rewards upon the innately gifted. The best of all distributive systems was one in which 'social inequalities express precisely natural inequalities' (D 313).

In the good society, the division of labour would be as unforced as it was possible to make it; only when the abnormal forms were eliminated would the moral foundations be in place for a genuinely solidary society. Where the division of labour lacked spontaneity, coercion of one kind or another was being used, so undermining the basis for normative consensus. Durkheim is not very forthcoming on the details of social engineering required to end the forced division of labour. But he is quite clear that drastic changes were called for and that these were a prior condition of any reordering of moral and social principles. He thus believed, with Weber and *contra* Marx, that a normative system could not be imposed upon a society by coercion or ideological sleight of hand. For a set of values to be given broad endorsement there would have to be what Weber called an 'elective affinity' between the moral ideas and the social circumstances of those on the receiving end.

Commitment to the normative order could be regarded as somewhat problematic in the case of the least favoured members of society, those classes or strata among whom rebellious sentiments might find a receptive audience. Durkheim believed, in common with other liberal theorists of justice before and since, that socially inferior groups would be willing to accept their humble status if they could be convinced of its rational foundation. The lower orders either rebelled or accepted their lot with sullen resentment when the system was unfair and seen to be so. They would not feel the same way if the rules of the game were such that those who ended up at the bottom of the pile did so as a result of their own personal shortcomings and not because they had been denied opportunities available to others. Any system of constraints that was 'normal' in this sense would not need to use the heavy hand of coercion or rely on 'artful machination' to win compliance. To persuade the individual to 'submit to it of his own free will, there is no need to resort to deception. It is sufficient to make him aware of his natural state of dependence and inferiority.' Anyone capable of reason and reflection is able to see the benefits he receives by virtue of membership in society, and therefore accepts the need for social discipline as a price worth paying (R 143). The fact that some people may be more subordinate than others and have a heavier price to pay would not, one must assume, lead them to reflect unfavourably on their lot. Durkheim placed a lot of faith in people's willingness to bear burdens provided they could see themselves as part of some meaningful and just design. His entire theory of the division of labour as the basis of solidarity depended upon the general readiness to make such a connection. If individuals saw their daily toil in isolation, rather than as one important element in a purposeful whole, social solidarity would be sabotaged by the

64

division of labour, a point he emphasized when discussing another of its abnormal forms.

One of the difficulties he encountered in his analysis was how to reconcile his theory of the division of labour as a force for progress with the alienating effects of excessive specialization. Ever since Adam Smith, economists and social theorists had agonized about the dehumanizing consequences of routine and repetitive work. Comte had gone so far as to see the division of labour as a force driving mankind in the opposite direction, morally and socially, to that marked out for it by Durkheim. Workers reduced to the status of robots were not the stuff of which civilized society was made. What kind of solidarity could *they* be expected to engender?

In pondering the question, Durkheim seems prepared to acknowledge that when labour becomes ever more divided it does eventually have negative effects. He concedes that 'no matter how one represents the moral ideal, one cannot remain indifferent to such a debasement of human nature. If the aim of morality is individual perfection, it cannot allow the individual to be so utterly ruined . . .' (D 307). It had sometimes been suggested that the worst effects of alienation could be mitigated by ensuring that workers were given a liberal education, but Durkheim thought that this would only exacerbate the problem. Minds which had feasted on the delights of high culture would never thereafter be content with a starvation diet.

Durkheim's own solution to the problem was to deny that there was a problem. Extreme specialization, he contended, only produces deleterious effects in rare and exceptional cases. For the most part, the division of labour did not dehumanize workers because, however humdrum and repetitive their tasks, they were conscious of being part of a collective social enterprise, a co-operative activity which gave even the humblest operative a sense of involvement and purpose. He is 'not therefore a machine who repeats movements the sense of which he does not perceive, but he knows that they are tending in a certain direction, towards a goal that he can conceive of more or less distinctly. He feels that he is of some use' and that 'his actions have a goal beyond themselves.' The goal is the creation of social solidarity (D 308). Durkheim must be talking about the division of labour after it has

65

been purged of all its forced or abnormal features, when careers are fully open to all the talents and rewards conform to the dictates of social justice. Under these conditions, even the most routine of tasks will be invested with a new meaning, a moral significance which is not inherent in the task itself, but which is imparted to it by a common consciousness inspired by the spirit of justice. Critics of the division of labour thus draw the wrong conclusions because they focus narrowly on the work activity itself and so ignore the moral framework in which it takes place and which endows it with its true significance.

II

The fact that Durkheim was less than happy with the existing social order would naturally have caused him to contemplate the socialist alternative. Many of his closest colleagues were politically left of centre, and his own teachings about solidarity and collectivism had a certain resonance with socialist ideas. His detractors often regarded him as a man of the Left and several of his biographers have depicted him as a socialist of sorts. However, the fact that he has also been dubbed a conservative and a proto-Fascist, among other things, suggests that his political preferences cannot easily be pigeon-holed. If he did harbour firm socialist convictions he managed to conceal them quite effectively in his lectures on the movement and its ideology. In the light of what he had to say about socialism, his refusal to join the movement or to identify openly with its aims must have come as an enormous relief to the party bosses.

In his lectures on socialism, given towards the end of the nineteenth century, he adopts the posture of a medical man called in to diagnose a strange and worrying illness. Socialism is examined as the symptom of a disease; its very appearance is a sure sign that society is sick. Socialism, he writes, is 'a cry of grief, sometimes of anger, uttered by men who feel most keenly our collective malaise. Socialism is to the facts which produce it what the groans of a sick man are to the illness with which he is afflicted.' (SSS 41) There is a faint echo here of Marx's definition of religion as 'the sigh of the oppressed creature, the heart of a heartless world' (MER 38).

Socialism for Durkheim, like religion for Marx, was not itself an ailment but an external sign or symptom of an underlying malady. Society would have to be cured before socialism would go away. Seen in this way, socialism is functionally equivalent to suicide. A high or abnormal suicide rate sends out the same kind of warning signals to the organism as the presence of a socialist movement. The remedial steps taken to ensure that fewer people kill themselves should at the same time bring about the demise of socialism. The appropriate treatment for both is good social hygiene.

Given Durkheim's usual way of reasoning, it is somewhat paradoxical that he should treat suicide and socialism, by implication at least, as equivalent social facts. The paradox arises because he generally sets great store by the virtues of group solidarity and moral cohesion. As we have earlier seen, he argued that the most effective antidote against egoistic suicide was the close integration of the individual in a moral community—any kind of community would do, provided that it gave its members a firm social anchorage. At the time Durkheim was writing, the labour movement and socialist parties were among the few organizations which could provide industrial workers and the urban poor with a sense of community and self-esteem. Socialist parties often resembled societies in miniature, havens in which the dispossessed could find a modicum of comfort and shelter from the chill blasts of capitalism. They were, in brief, exactly the kind of moral communities whose prophylactic qualities Durkheim recommended. The conclusion should have been clear: socialism stops you from killing yourself.

It is not as if Durkheim was blind to the integrative appeal of socialism. Far from it; he singles this out as the movement's concealed rationale. The demands for social equality and material betterment were secondary or peripheral aspects of socialism. The heart of the doctrine, and the movement's *raison d'être*, was the desire for full incorporation of the working class into civil society.

In other words, according to socialism there is presently an entire segment of the economic world which is not truly and directly integrated into society. This is the working class, not the capitalists. They are not fully-fledged members of society, since they participate in the community's life only through an imposed medium which, having its own nature, prevents them from acting upon society and receiving benefits from it in a measure and manner consistent with the social value of their services. It is this which creates the situation they are said to suffer from. What they desire, consequently, when they demand better treatment, is to be no longer kept at a distance from the centres presiding over collective life but be bound to them more or less intimately. The material changes they hope for are only one form and result of this more complete integration. (SSS 60–1)

On Durkheim's reading of the movement, then, socialism is primarily a plea for the assimilation of workers into capitalism, rather than for a new society founded on different principles. This interpretation is similar to that of Lenin and other revolutionaries who castigated the movement's leaders for showing more enthusiasm for entering into partnership with the bourgeoisie than for liquidating it. But however consistent such a view may be with the tenets of Leninism, in the context of Durkheimian sociology it is extremely anomalous for an organization to be defined principally in terms of its integrative functions and at the same time to be diagnosed as a pathological symptom.

The most likely reason for this negative evaluation is that socialism was the collective representation of a particular social class, not of society as a whole. Durkheim felt that it would be a 'considerable step forward ... if socialism finally abandoned confusing the social question with that of the workers ... The malaise from which we are suffering is not rooted in any particular class. It attacks employers as well as workers, although it manifests itself in different forms in both ...' (G 142–3). Socialism, because of its class orientation, disturbed the moral equilibrium; it was a source of schism rather than solidarity. There could only be one Church in society, one overarching value system, and this was always the creation of the total society, not one of its parts.

Interestingly, some of Durkheim's ideas concerning solidarity could be employed in a manner uncongenial to his own thesis. The notions that he applies indiscriminately to 'society' acquire a good deal more force when applied to specific interest groups or

68

collectivities such as classes. His discussion of the moral transformation brought about by sacred ceremonies, and the role of ritual and symbolism in fostering social solidarity, could be read as an account of the way in which social classes and status groups develop a sense of self-awareness and common identity. It could in other words be seen as an attempt to show the process by which classes 'in themselves' become classes 'for themselves'. The cultural and symbolic aspects of class did not feature prominently in the socialist theories of his time, and had he chosen to exploit his own insights he might have gone some way towards explaining why the working class did not always act in accordance with the expectations of socialist doctrine. The French Marxists who later took up this question, the structuralists in particular, ignored Durkheim's ideas completely, partly no doubt because his conceptual vocabulary could not easily have been incorporated into the exoteric idiom of Althusserian discourse.

In electing not to delve too deeply into matters of class, material or symbolic, Durkheim's analysis of socialism runs true to form. Where, however, it marks a departure from his usual strategy is in the treatment of doctrine. Generally speaking, he is quite indifferent to the actual content or substance of beliefs. His theory of religion, for example, pays little heed to the cosmology of totemism, by comparison with the forms and practices of ritual. Durkheim's religious actors behave the way they do because of the social imperatives which propel them this way and that, not because of the nature of their beliefs. Catholics kill themselves less often than Protestants not because of doctrinal differences between the two religions, but because their Churches are socially organized along contrasting lines. The content of belief is of small importance because the primary function of religion is to unite its adherents into a single moral community virtually any set of beliefs will do for this purpose. Besides, picking away at the meaning of doctrine is a task for the theologian, not the social theorist.

Socialism stands out as the exception. This is one set of beliefs which Durkheim does feel bound to examine under the microscope. He discovers a number of flaws in the system, not the least of them being socialism's erroneous view of human nature and its misguided conception of distributive justice. Socialism misunder-

69

stands human nature because it promotes the belief that full self-realization will only be attained when the institutional fetters created by society are torn away. Society is presented as an artificial device, a set of obstacles standing between the individual and his human capacities. The truth is the very opposite of this. Social institutions and the constraints they impose upon us are the things that make us free. It is the state of nature which enslaves mankind, and release from this condition can only come about by the continuous encroachments of society. Human happiness and fulfilment was predicated on the existence of powerful social bonds, but socialism made the error of confusing bonds with bondage. It was a cruel and self-defeating doctrine because it raised general expectations to a level it could not hope to meet. No sooner would one set of wants be satisfied than a dozen new ones would be unleashed. This endless stimulation of desires was fatal to social stability. 'What is needed if social order is to reign is that the mass of men be content with their lot. But what is needed for them to be content, is not that they have more or less but that they be convinced they have no right to more.' (SSS 242) Socialism sought to convince people of the opposite; it had no taste for the moral discipline and self-restraint that kept the forces of anarchy at bay.

Durkheim's critique does touch upon a weak spot in socialist theory, one that has become more apparent in our day than it was in his. The good society of socialist dreams was one flowing with abundance. The new order would not simply distribute goods and resources more fairly than capitalism did, it would also produce them in greater quantity. Plenty would take the place of scarcity by the reorganization of production along more rational lines and by the release of human energies which had been bottled up or frittered away under capitalism.

Seen from the vantage point of the late twentieth century, the optimism of the early socialists appears a little quaint. Few of the committed would today hold out the prospect of a socialist cornucopia to come. The language of relative scarcity has replaced that of abundance as all social systems, real and imagined, confront the possibility of diminishing resources. It is in this moral climate that Durkheim's ideas take on a new lease of life. He, more than any other social theorist, poses the awkward questions about the need for voluntary constraint—how to get people to accept less than they have been accustomed to or less than they feel they are entitled to. The scaling down of expectations on a voluntary basis presupposes a broad moral consensus on the criteria of distribution. Such a consensus does not drop from the skies, nor can it be imposed upon a reluctant society. There is little in socialist theory or practice to indicate that it contains the answer to the problem.

Although the language of self-discipline and restraint may be appropriate to certain social situations, it seems doubtful whether Durkheim's use of it as a stick with which to beat the early socialists was altogether warranted. The late nineteenth century does not readily come to mind as a period in which the mass of the population was drunk with ambition and limitless aspirations. The gaze of the urban poor would have been fixed at a point a good deal nearer their feet than some far distant horizon. The material and mental condition of the working class as depicted in Zola's *Germinal* is difficult to reconcile with Durkheim's anxieties about their insatiable wants. As socialist agitators of the time could no doubt have informed him, the problem was not how to dampen down wild hopes for a better life, but how to combat the anaesthetizing effects of apathy and fatalism. The socialists who read Durkheim must have wondered where all that combustible material was hiding.

In his proposals for the moral education of the young, Durkheim betrays the same needless concern. No distinction is drawn between the levels of motivation of advantaged and disadvantaged groups; the children of rich and poor alike are caught up in the same unseemly urge to make good. 'Because, in principle, all vocations are available to everybody, the drive to get ahead is more readily stimulated and inflamed beyond all measure to the point of knowing almost no limits.' (ME 49) One of the main purposes of education was therefore to curb this tendency. A disciplinary regime was called for which would 'teach the child to rein in his desires, to set limits to his appetites of all kinds' (ME 43).

Had Durkheim been more familiar with the cultural aspects of class society, he would have recognized that the repression of ambition was a common defensive strategy among the poor and

71

did not need to be taught as part of the school curriculum. This is one of the dysfunctional aspects of a stratified system; low-status groups scale down their children's aspirations, and so the talent they have available cannot be exploited to the full. This, in other words, was why the division of labour remained 'forced' and why social inequalities failed to correspond to natural inequalities. One of the most formidable obstacles to the attainment of Durkheim's meritocratic ideal would have been an educational system inspired by his own pedagogy. Socialism, by seeking to raise the sights of the common people, was probably more consistent with meritocracy than a schoolroom regime centred around the need for 'limits', 'discipline', 'checks', and 'constraint'.

Durkheim was perhaps less sensitive to the meritocratic potential of socialism than he might have been because of his concern about its egalitarian impulse. Socialist equality was no improvement on market distribution, and might even be worse. To distribute rewards equally, irrespective of differences in effort or social worth, was as indefensible as allocation by the lottery of supply and demand. Moreover, an egalitarian society would have to use the heavy hand of coercion, because the talented and industrious would never willingly accept the same level of reward as that given to the feckless and work-shy (S 278–9). Under such conditions moral consensus could never be established, with all that that implied in the way of chronic instability. Durkheim never lived to see socialism put into practice. He died shortly after the Bolsheviks seized power, though perhaps too much should not be read into that. Had he ever had the opportunity to study what came to be known by the bizarre name of 'actually existing socialism', it is unlikely that he would have felt compelled to revise his original opinion of the doctrine.

5 State and civil society

I

In Durkheim's earliest writings, the state is a rather shadowy institution, an agency that performs certain tasks of co-ordination without having a distinct character of its own. Even when certain types of state are identified by name it is usually to minimize their explanatory importance. In his dissertation on Montesquieu, Durkheim gently chided his predecessor for following the conventional practice of classifying societies according to the nature of the sovereign power. He argued that political concepts such as Monarchy, Aristocracy, Despotism, Democracy, and the like were irrelevant to the understanding of society. Social structure had a reality of its own which endowed it with a long-term continuity, whereas the state was a transient and conditional affair. 'The form of government does not determine the nature of a society. As we have shown, the nature of the supreme power can be modified while the social structure remains unchanged, or conversely it can remain identical in societies which differ in the extreme.' (MR 33) The two basic forms of social structure, mechanical and organic solidarity, were each compatible with a variety of political superstructures. Absolutism, for example, could be found both in simple and complex societies. It is not therefore 'a consequence of the fundamental nature of the society, but rather depends on unique, transitory and contingent factors' (T 288). France was a monarchical despotism in the seventeenth century and a liberal republic in the nineteenth century, but the essential character of French society remained the same throughout. Unlike the state, a society 'can no more change its type in the course of its evolution than can an animal change its species during its own lifetime' (T 288). The violent transition from, say, the Tsarist autocracy to the dictatorship of the proletariat would thus cause little more than a ripple on the surface of Russian society.

Unusually for him, Durkheim was not altogether consistent in his evaluation of the state. In the *Division of Labour*, the state

73

is alluded to as a 'central organ' whose primary purpose is to co-ordinate the functions of the various parts of the system. This central organ comes to life only as society becomes more complex. Under mechanical solidarity it is only present in embryonic form, since there are relatively few separate functions for it to oversee. When labour becomes divided it assumes a more recognizable shape, but it never takes on a dominant role. Even in the most advanced society, the central organ is not the prime mover; it is one part among many and makes no deep impress upon the whole.

In his later writings, the *Leçons de sociologie* (1950) in particular, Durkheim allows the modern state to play a more prominent role. In certain respects, but not all, he adopts the standard liberal view of the state as an organ which stands 'above' society, a politically neutral force which acts impartially for the common good. He was temperamentally averse to the Marxist notion of the state as an executive committee of the ruling class. This kind of terminology was outside his moral wavelength and, besides, it jarred too much with his conception of the modern state as the embodiment of rationality. In fact, he tended to invest the state with almost quasi-mystical properties, rather in the manner of Hegel. For Hegel, it was through the state that individuals attained full consciousness of themselves as sentient moral beings; the state was the highest and most perfect manifestation of the human spirit.

For Durkheim, it was society which was the main beneficiary of the state's extraordinary cognitive powers. The state was possessed of a special kind of consciousness, one that was quite different from the common consciousness that emanated from civil society. The common consciousness was really an amalgam of 'feelings, desires, and beliefs which society has worked out collectively and which are diffused throughout all consciences' (L 113). Folklore, myth, custom, and tradition were the source of this mishmash of ideas. The consciousness located in the state, on the other hand, was far more refined, one that was 'narrower but higher and clearer and with a sharper sense of itself' (L 86). The state was the organ of rational thought, the seat of an intelligence blessed with the capacity for reflection and calm deliberation. Its principal function was to think.

In pressing the distinction between the common consciousness of civil society and the higher intelligence of the state, Durkheim draws an analogy with the mind. At the subconscious level, the human psyche is a rag-bag of passions and sentiments which are of obscure origin and have little to do with deliberate reflection. Our behaviour is often affected by these sentiments, yet at the same time we react against them by seeking to understand the reasons for our actions. We do this by drawing upon the rational core of our psyche, the inner circle which is the repository of reflective thought. We seek, in other words, to attain self-mastery by bringing the passions under the control of our intellects. The rational core of the mind stands in the same relationship to the subconscious as the intelligence of the state does to the common consciousness of civil society (L 113–14).

The implication is clear enough. Durkheim is saying that civil society needs the state to think on its behalf because the common consciousness is not up to the job. Left to its own devices, civil society would be in danger of sliding back into a state of nature, just as an individual lacking the ability to reason would be brought low by his own untamed passions. The state saves civil society from itself.

This conception of the state as reason personified is a far cry from the classical liberal view. Liberal theorists do not generally claim that the purpose of the state is to think on behalf of society. The state should keep its nose out of people's affairs. Surprisingly, perhaps, Durkheim's notion of the state as an organ of higher intelligence bears a certain resemblance to one variant of the Marxist view. Structural Marxists argue that one of the duties of the bourgeois state is to think and plan on behalf of the capitalist class. The suggestion is that capitalists are unable to pursue their own long-term interests as a class because they are too preoccupied with their immediate, short-term interests as individuals. They therefore need the state to act on their behalf. Because the bourgeois state is not directly caught up in the day-to-day struggle between the classes it is able to take a more detached and rational view of the capitalists' collective interests than are the capitalists themselves. What is rational economic activity for any one capitalist (the maximum exploitation of labour) is irrational for capitalists as a class (because of the threat

75

of a workers' revolt). The task of the state is thus to blunt the sharp edges of the system and make it more palatable to the dangerous classes. The state uses its higher reason to save the bourgeoisie from itself.

Where the parallel between Durkheimian and Marxist views breaks down is in Durkheim's predictable claim that the state thinks on behalf of the whole society, not just one of its parts. Neither view, however, addresses the question of who exactly are the intellectual supermen in the service of the state. The assumption in both cases appears to be that the incumbency of state office is in itself the guarantee of higher rationality, quite irrespective of the mental capacities of the flesh-and-blood officials. Sweep out one set of officials and replace them with a new lot and the kingdom of reason would be unimpaired. The rationality of state, rather like the suicide rate, has a reality of its own, beyond the messy interference of human subjects.

Presenting the state in this way appears to dispose of the awkward problem of bureaucracy. Bureaucrats have a way of using, or abusing, their authority to feather their own nest. Had Durkheim directed his attention to the incumbents of state, he would have faced the difficulty of explaining why they would choose to use the rational powers at their disposal for the benefit of all rather than for their own sectional advantage. The state could only perform its high-minded role if the people running the show were selected not so much for their intellects as for their altruism.

Durkheim does seem to be aware of the possibility of the state misusing its powers. There was always a danger that it could invade the domain of civil society and curtail the rights of the individual. In order to safeguard against this it was essential to have a dense layer of intermediate groups between the state and the individual, a set of institutions which could serve as a buffer to shield the citizen against an overbearing central power. Civil society could best play this protective role if the intermediate groups in question were of a specific kind—namely, professional associations or occupational guilds. Durkheim believed that these groups were ideally suited to serve as the building-blocks of civil society on a number of grounds. In the first place, they arose from the division of labour and were therefore rooted in the most elemental feature of modern society. They were also moral communities in the most complete sense. As a member of an occupational group, each individual enjoyed a strong sense of personal worth; it was the milieu in which the average person spent most of his active life, and the daily contact with others engaged in the same profession forged a powerful set of social bonds and common sentiments. In short, the occupational guild was the basis of social solidarity in the modern age.

Durkheim's enthusiasm for this form of social organization appears to have been fuelled by his understanding of the medieval guilds. These were close-knit groups of workmen and artisans which regulated almost all aspects of their members' lives. Similar guilds had also existed in Roman society, often associated with a religious cult. Durkheim was evidently impressed by the moral energy which the guilds displayed and by their highly developed sense of collective identity. He reasoned that if these bodies had developed spontaneously throughout different periods of history they must be possessed of a timeless authenticity and a functional importance which could answer to present-day needs. This is not to say that he was advocating the revival of medieval guilds. He recognized that they had fallen into decay because of internal corruption and their inability to adapt to changing circumstances. What he wished for was a type of guild that had a natural compatibility with modern industrialism.

The new guilds would be quite different from trade unions. Durkheim was not too keen on unions; he was inclined to see them as selfish organizations, always prepared to put their members' interests above the common good. Employers' organizations were just as bad. The conflict between the groups representing capital and labour was wholly destructive, a civil war waged without the restraining hand of a shared morality. The new guilds would put an end to the strife by reining in their members' demands and inculcating the habit of self-discipline. Durkheim believed that individuals yearned to have a strong framework of rules which marked out the limits of their actions and banished the temptations of excess. A life of contentment was only attainable when social goals were moderated and brought into line with the means for achieving them. The guilds would be the instrument for bringing about this alignment, so satisfying both the individual's craving for moral regulation and society's need for tranquillity.

Durkheim is characteristically vague when it comes to the organizational structure of the guilds. He indicates only that they should elect representatives to national assemblies and tribunals charged with the task of regulating industry and employment. Workers and employers should each be represented on these various bodies.

> The proportion of each should correspond to the respective importance attributed by public opinion to these two factors of production. But if it is necessary for both sides to meet on the governing councils of the corporation it is no less indispensable for them to constitute distinct and independent groups at the lower level of corporative organisation, because too often their interests vie with one another and are opposing. To feel that they exist freely, they must be aware of their separate existence. The two bodies so constituted can then appoint their representatives to the common assemblies. (D lix)

It seems from this that the guild or corporative set-up was intended to bring harmony between capital and labour at the highest decision-making level, while allowing their antagonism in the workplace to have free expression. Durkheim was thus assuming, not unrealistically, that the incorporation of 'workers' leaders or representatives into the power structure of industry would have a mollifying effect on labour relations. This is a rare admission that the key to the problem of order might lie in the conduct of élites rather than that of the population as a whole.

In addition to their role as moral and industrial regulators, Durkheim also expected the guilds to assume heavy political responsibilities. He proposed that the electorate should cast its vote not as residents of this or that territorial constituency, but as members of an occupation or profession. He felt that place of residence was a poor basis upon which to mobilize political opinion. Because of the upsurge of geographical mobility in modern society, individuals no longer had a deep attachment to place or locality. Electoral units based upon towns and districts were therefore artificial constructs, mere administrative devices lacking any social significance. Guilds, on the other hand, were genuine moral communities; they embraced fully the lives of their members and were the vehicles best fitted to express the citizens' true interests. This being so, everyone should vote as a member of an occupational group.

The reason that Durkheim was so taken with this idea was that he had a rather odd notion of the purpose of the franchise. In liberal democratic theory, the vote is seen as an expression of the political will of the individual; it is the means by which each person passes judgement upon the performance of government. It is essentially a private affair, hence the requirement that it take place in the secrecy of the polling booth. This individualist conception of voting is anathema to Durkheim. If everyone registers his political choice 'in isolation, it is virtually impossible that such votes would be motivated by anything other than personal and egoistic concerns', with the result that 'individualistic particularism' would be the unsound basis of all political organization (L 138). Durkheim invites us to contrast this unsatisfactory arrangement with one in which voting takes place under the benign influence of the collectivity. When 'men think in common their thought is, in part, the work of the community. The community acts upon them, weighs down upon them with all its authority, restrains their egoistic desires and directs their minds towards a collective end.' (L 138) To vote as a member of an occupational guild would encourage each person to reflect upon the broader interest, rather than indulge in political whim and individual fancy. He does not go so far as to recommend that voting should take place in public, by a show of hands, though that would be the most effective way of ensuring that personal political inclinations were suppressed in favour of group conformity.

Durkheim managed to combine a disdain for 'individualistic particularism' at the ballot box with a fervent commitment to individualism as a political philosophy. When the battle lines were drawn in the Dreyfus affair, he aligned himself publicly with the Dreyfusards on the grounds that the rights of the individual took precedence over *raisons d'État*. To sacrifice an innocent man on the altar of a hypothetical national interest would be to strike at the very heart of individualism—the new religion of humanity and the only moral code by which a modern society could live.

The anti-Dreyfusards had fallen into the error of equating individualism with egoism; whereas egoism was truly destructive of collective life, giving vent as it did to selfish and anti-social impulses, individualism was the pinnacle of moral evolution, a celebration of the rights of man and a lodestar of any good society in the making. To confuse individualism with egoism was rather like equating God with Satan. (I)

The trouble with individuals, however, is that they are often prone to think and do things in their capacity as individuals, thereby taking the first step on the slippery slope to egoism. Durkheim seems much more comfortable with the notion of the individual as a bundle of rights than as a political or social actor. The individual considered as a bundle of rights has a certain moral grandeur by dint of the fact that the rights in question are a gift from society, the fount of all virtue. But when this same individual goes to the ballot box he becomes a social actor, and in the privacy of the polling booth he is able to register a personal choice free from the watchful eye of the community. In this artificial setting he is all too likely to allow his own predilections to get the better of him; entering the booth as an individual, he comes out as an egoist. Durkheim must have thought how much more satisfactory it would be if people would rest content with the possession of individual rights and not persist in the irritating habit of putting them into practice.

II

A political system organized around occupational guilds would effectively disenfranchise those people not engaged in the paid division of labour. In Durkheim's day, this would have included the majority of women, so that on his formula civil society would have been a predominantly male society. This might not have given him undue pause for thought since his views about women were not exactly in advance of their time. He felt that women were creatures of nature, whereas men were products of society. Man is actively involved in social affairs; he is more fully social-ized than woman, his pulse beats to the vibrant rhythms of col-lective life. Woman, being locked in the drab routine of domestic life, is barely touched by the stimulating currents of society and culture. She remains a creature of instinct and impulse, while man is reason made flesh (S 443). If the common consciousness had a gender it would be female, just as the higher rationality of the state would be male.

Durkheim, in a departure from his usual mode of reasoning, does not suggest that the differences between the sexes are attributable to their different social functions, and could therefore be dissolved or reduced by improving the status of women. He does not propose, for example, that inequality between the sexes could be lessened by incorporating women more fully into the division of labour; nor does he suggest that woman's nature would become more like man's once women did the same jobs as men. In fact, he predicted that differences between the sexes would widen rather than diminish over time. Women would certainly become more socialized than they are at present, but the irreducible inner core of femaleness would survive intact. Women would become social in their own distinctive way. They might, for example, take on the more aesthetic tasks, leaving men to concentrate on the technical side of things. Even with a completely free choice, women would still be drawn to those professions which were more congenial to the female temperament (S 443).

On the question of political rights also, Durkheim was a good deal more cautious in outlook than many contemporary liberals. He argued that, because of their unsocialized natures, women were not quite ready to enjoy the same rights as men. Radicals who demand equal rights for women immediately 'forget that the work of centuries cannot be undone at a stroke; moreover, equality before the law cannot be just while psychological inequality is so glaring' (S 444). When Durkheim trumpeted the rights of man, it was the rights of man he meant. To be granted the same legal and political rights as men, women would first need to be raised to the same mental and moral level as men. This sounds like a later version of John Stuart Mill's argument against enfranchising the working class; not until the workers had been educated and trained in the ways of civil society would they be fit to receive the gift of democracy.

Although Durkheim felt more or less the same way about the female franchise that Mill felt about the working-class franchise, he did not explicitly advocate the educational advancement of women as a means of narrowing the gap between the sexes. In his influential treatise on moral education, all his homilies relate to the instruction of young males; members of the opposite sex do not figure. Education apart, he offers no social programme for the amelioration of women's lot, no proposals for structural reform equivalent to the abolition of inherited wealth or the forced division of labour. Despite his fierce objection to unfair contracts, he does not ask whether inequality between the sexes is an example of this unfairness. Hypnotized by apparent differences in male and female temperaments, he is blind to the glaring imbalance of power between the sexes, an imbalance which men might be anxious to maintain, as would befit the paragons of rationality. Perhaps even Durkheim himself might have had a vested interest in seeing to it that Mme Durkheim remained a creature of instinct and nature instead of a pretender to the throne of reason.

III

As we have seen, Durkheim portrays the state as the 'brain' of society, a higher intelligence dedicated to the service of the community. Yet this same organ also represented a threat to society and the individual. The state could quite easily snuff out the flame of liberty by invading the territory that properly belonged to civil society. Durkheim argued that this was less likely to occur if civil society was built on solid foundations, the kind of institutional bedrock that only the occupational guilds were capable of putting in place. The individual needed civil society as protection against a heavy-handed state; but the state was also the creator and champion of individual liberty. The state should not be seen as 'an opponent of the individual. Individualism is not possible without it . . . It is the state which has shielded the child against patriarchal domination and family tyranny; it is the state which has emancipated the citizen from feudal and communal bonds; it is the state which has released the artisan and his master from the tyranny of the guilds . . .' and so on (L 99).

This bears more than a passing resemblance to Hegel's conception of the state as a liberating force through which mankind attains its highest moral destiny. Both theorists seem to have been carried away by their own enthusiasm. To take Durkheim's examples, the liberation of the artisan and master from guild tyranny, or the freeing of the peasantry from feudal overlords, probably had more to do with economic changes, the quickening of market relations in particular, than with the actions of a benevolent state. The absolutist states which ruled at the time were not well known for their attachment to individual rights and liberties; monarchs who ruled by divine right and who looked upon their people as subjects rather than citizens would seem to be an improbable source of emancipation. Far from being the prime mover in the expansion of liberty, the state generally appears to have been something of a laggard, giving belated recognition to changes which had already taken place outside its orbit.

Perhaps all that Durkheim meant to say was that individual liberties only become fully secured and guaranteed once they have received the state's imprimatur. It would then be plausible to claim that the state is a *sine qua non* of rights and liberties. Even so, this should not be taken to mean that the state in general necessarily serves the cause of liberty in this way. Some states do, some do not. Durkheim commonly speaks of the 'state' in an ideal-typical sense, instead of this or that particular form or type of state; indeed, he openly disclaims the sociological relevance of any classification based on different types of sovereign power. Aristocracy, despotism, democracy; strawberry, chocolate, and vanilla. Had he been readier to concede that different forms of state could be just as consequential as different forms of social solidarity, he could have gone on to situate the discussion of rights and liberties in the comparative political framework that is clearly called for.

The lack of such a framework also tends to vitiate his otherwise subtle analysis of the relationship between the modern state and civil society. He points out that the intermediate groups that constitute civil society—above all, the occupational guilds—may themselves be tempted to act in a domineering way towards their members. If their powers were left unchecked they could make prisoners of free men. It was therefore the duty of the state to intercede on behalf of the individual to prevent his rights being nullified by civil society or one of its constituent parts (L 98). As

83

Durkheim sees it, then, there is a complex dialectic between the individual, civil society, and the state. Civil society serves to protect the individual against the predatory power of the state, while this same power is mobilized in defence of individual liberty against the incursions of civil society. This comes about because state and civil society each has a Jekyll-and-Hyde character; the malevolent side of one is neutralized by the benevolent side of the other. 'It is from this opposition of social forces that individual liberties are born.' (L 99)

The assumption underlying Durkheim's model is that state and civil society enjoy roughly equal amounts of power; if either one were in a position to dominate the other, the political tension or balance between them would be upset, with grim consequences for individual liberty. In the real world, however, such a delicate equilibrium is rarely if ever found. The state, by definition, is the supreme or sovereign power, and as such it claims jurisdiction over all other institutions. Civil society is very much the junior partner in this relationship and would not be much of a match for a Leviathan that was bent on punching its weight to the full. If the state refrains from usurping the powers vested in civil society, this is because it elects to do so; it is a voluntary relinquishment of power. The rights and liberties which the state grants today could be withdrawn tomorrow if the state so determined. How much freedom of manœuvre is bestowed upon civil society, and how secure or precarious that freedom would prove to be, is thus ultimately dependent upon the political character of the state. Because different types of regime allow different degrees of latitude to civil society, the question of individual liberty calls for a comparative approach, and hence for the very kind of political typology that Durkheim felt to be beneath sociological consideration.

This is not to deny that his conception of civil society is extremely pertinent to an understanding of the modern democratic state. He is, in effect, suggesting that intermediate social groups perform the valuable role of creating a culture of democracy: that is, a matrix of norms, practices, and assumptions which are vital to the operation of a formally democratic polity. As Durkheim sees it, democracy as a system of legal institutions needs to be both sustained and complemented by the civic virtues that arise within the intimate, miniature societies which flourish outside the ordinary compass of the state. A vigorous civil society is likely to insinuate its own good habits into the institutions of the state, thereby reducing the potential for friction between citizens and the sovereign power. The state could still, in theory, trump any of the cards held by other independent social bodies, but the civilizing effect of these bodies is to lessen the state's impulse to act overbearingly. Hence, in Western democracies today, the military arm of the state retains the capacity to sub-jugate civil society by force, but the fact that it rarely if ever seeks to do so suggests that the men on horseback have themselves come to endorse the democratic ethos propagated by civil society. The state may be the stronger partner, measured by the indices of physical power, but civil society can make up for what it lacks in this department by its exercise of moral authority. As Durkheim properly insists, moral authority can often be every bit as potent as main force in setting the limits to social action.

In seeking to locate the underpinnings of modern democracy, Durkheim was tackling head on a problem that both Marx and Weber chose to ignore. For Marx, of course, the notion of democracy was just another bourgeois confidence trick, a device for obscuring the factual disparity of power between unequal classes. There could, moreover, be no valid distinction between state and civil society because the former was simply the instrument which enforced the hegemony of the latter—civil society being no more than a fancy name for the dictatorship of the bourgeoisie. Not surprisingly, political regimes inspired by Marx's teachings have shown no qualms about dissolving civil society altogether, so exposing their subjects to the full blast of state power.

Weber, too, had little to say about the social conditions con-ducive to a democratic order. Indeed, in some respects his political sociology can be read as a gloomy denial of the possibility of genuine democracy. To one who saw the unremitting advance of bureaucracy as the central fact of modernity, the notion of civil society would have seemed touchingly archaic, a futile harking back to a lost age of *Gemeinschaft*. The spirit and practice of democracy were wholly alien to the grim imperatives of bureau-cratic control, and in any contest between the two there could be no doubt that bureaucracy would emerge triumphant.

The difference here between Marx and Weber on the one hand,

and Durkheim on the other, is symptomatic of a more profound contrast of political temperaments. Durkheimian sociology is driven by a concern to identify pathologies in the body politic with a view to offering practical remedies. Western capitalist democracy is, for him, seriously defective in its moral and social arrangements; but it is nevertheless corrigible. It is quite capable of being altered in ways that are not trivial or illusory.

Marx and Weber, each in his different fashion, perceive the same system to be much less yielding to the reformist touch. All attempts to realign the structures of power are bound to come to grief on the hard reality of either capital or bureaucracy. For Marx, the only alternative is to bulldoze away the rubbish tip of history and start again from scratch. For Weber, such an alternative is laughable, but not much more so than any other proposal for bucking the bureaucratic trend. However soulless and stultifying it may be, the iron cage of bureaucratic domination is here to stay, and all talk of breaking free of it is so much empty twaddle.

Against Marx's messianic utopianism, and Weber's counsel of despair, Durkheim holds out the fair prospect of orderly social change and steady moral progress. His cautious optimism should be congenial to those decent and generous spirits who believe that Western society is sufficiently malleable to make the effort at reform worthwhile and that the system still has quite a long way to go before its potential is finally exhausted.

Bibliography and suggestions for further reading

The English versions of *Le Suicide*, *Les Formes élémentaires de la vie religieuse*, and *Leçons de sociologie* are not satisfactory and the translations in the text are my own.

BIBLIOGRAPHIC DETAILS OF WORKS CITED

Works by Émile Durkheim: *The Division of Labour in Society* (Paris, 1893), trans. W. D. Halls (London, 1984); *The Rules of Sociological Method* (Paris, 1895), trans. W. D. Halls (London, 1982); *Le Suicide* (Paris, 1897; Presses Universitaires de France, Paris, 1990), trans. J. A. Spaulding and G. Simpson (Glencoe, 1951); *Les Formes élémentaires de la vie religieuse* (Paris, 1912; Presses Universitaires de France, Paris, 1990), trans. J. W. Swain (London, 1915); *Leçons de sociologie* (Istanbul, 1950; Presses Universitaires de France, Paris, 1990), trans. C. Brookfield, as *Professional Ethics and Civic Morals* (London, 1957); *Montesquieu and Rousseau* (Paris, 1953), trans. R. Manheim (Ann Arbor, 1960); *Moral Education* (Paris, 1925), trans. E. K. Wilson and H. Schnurer (New York, 1961); *Primitive Classification* (Paris, 1903), trans. R. Needham (London, 1963); *Socialism and Saint-Simon* (Paris, 1928), trans. C. Sattler (Yellow Springs, Ohio, 1958); 'Individualism and the Intellectuals' (Paris, 1898), trans. S. and J. Lukes, *Political Studies*, xvii (1969), 14–30; 'Two Laws of Penal Evolution' (Paris, 1901), trans. T. Jones and A. Scull, *Economy and Society*, ii (1973), 285–308.

Collected essays: *Durkheim: Essays on Morals and Education*, ed. W. S. F. Pickering (London, 1979); *Durkheim on Politics and the State*, ed. A. Giddens (Cambridge, 1986); *Durkheim on Religion*, ed. W. S. F. Pickering (London, 1975).

Other works cited: G. Davy, 'Émile Durkheim: L'Homme', *Revue de metaphysique et de morale*, xxvi (1919); J. Douglas, *The Social Meanings of Suicide* (Princeton, 1967); Sir J. Frazer, *The Golden Bough*, vol. i (London, 1911); R. A. Jones, *Émile Durkheim: An Introduction to Four Major Works* (Beverly Hills, Calif., 1986); S. M. Lukes, *Émile Durkheim: His Life and Work*,

(London, 1973); S. M. Lukes, 'Introduction' to Durkheim's *Rules of Sociological Method*, trans. W. D. Halls (London, 1982); K. Marx, *Capital*, vol. iii (Moscow, 1972); K. Marx, *Grundrisse*, ed. D. McLellan (London, 1971); K. Marx and F. Engels, *On Religion* (Moscow, 1957).

FURTHER READING

The 1988 edition of Steven Lukes's, *Émile Durkheim: His Life and Work*, contains a comprehensive bibliography of Durkheim's publications and Durkheimiana. First published in 1973, this remains the definitive work on the subject in any language. There are a number of brief expositions of Durkheim's sociology, of which the following may be recommended: A. Giddens, *Durkheim* (Glasgow, 1978); K. Thompson, *Émile Durkheim* (London, 1982); R. Nisbet, *The Sociology of Émile Durkheim* (New York, 1974). Nisbet's book presents Durkheim as a conservative thinker; for a contrary view the reader should turn to F. Pearce, *The Radical Durkheim* (London, 1989). Among specialist works, the following are of particular interest: M. Gane, *On Durkheim's Rules of Sociological Method* (London, 1988); V. Karady (ed.), *Textes*, 3 vols. (Paris, 1975); D. LaCapra, *Émile Durkheim: Sociologist and Philosopher* (Ithaca, 1972); B. Lacroix, *Durkheim et le politique* (Montreal, 1981); W. S. F. Pickering, *Durkheim's Sociology of Religion: Themes and Theories* (London, 1984); W. Pope, *Durkheim's* Suicide: *A Classic Analyzed* (Chicago, 1976); E. Wallwork, *Durkheim, Morality and Milieu* (Cambridge, Mass., 1972).

Index

Index

OXFORD

MORE OXFORD PAPERBACKS

This book is just one of nearly 1000 Oxford Paperbacks currently in print. If you would like details of other Oxford Paperbacks, including titles in the World's Classics, Oxford Reference, Oxford Books, OPUS, Past Masters, Oxford Authors, and Oxford Shakespeare series, please write to:

UK and Europe: Oxford Paperbacks Publicity Manager, Arts and Reference Publicity Department, Oxford University Press, Walton Street, Oxford OX2 6DP.

Customers in UK and Europe will find Oxford Paperbacks available in all good bookshops. But in case of difficulty please send orders to the Cash-with-Order Department, Oxford University Press Distribution Services, Saxon Way West, Corby, Northants NN18 9ES. Tel: 0536 741519; Fax: 0536 746337. Please send a cheque for the total cost of the books, plus £1.75 postage and packing for orders under £20; £2.75 for orders over £20. Customers outside the UK should add 10% of the cost of the books for postage and packing.

USA: Oxford Paperbacks Marketing Manager, Oxford University Press, Inc., 200 Madison Avenue, New York, N.Y. 10016.

Canada: Trade Department, Oxford University Press, 70 Wynford Drive, Don Mills, Ontario M3C 1J9.

Australia: Trade Marketing Manager, Oxford University Press, G.P.O. Box 2784Y, Melbourne 3001, Victoria.

South Africa: Oxford University Press, P.O. Box 1141, Cape Town 8000.

PAST MASTERS

General Editor: Keith Thomas

The *Past Masters* series offers students and general readers alike concise introductions to the lives and works of the world's greatest literary figures, composers, philosophers, religious leaders, scientists, and social and political thinkers.

'Put end to end, this series will constitute a noble encyclopaedia of the history of ideas.' Mary Warnock

HOBBES

Richard Tuck

Thomas Hobbes (1588–1679) was the first great English political philosopher, and his book *Leviathan* was one of the first truly modern works of philosophy. He has long had the reputation of being a pessimistic atheist, who saw human nature as inevitably evil, and who proposed a totalitarian state to subdue human failings. In this new study, Richard Tuck shows that while Hobbes may indeed have been an atheist, he was far from pessimistic about human nature, nor did he advocate totalitarianism. By locating him against the context of his age, Dr Tuck reveals Hobbs to have been passionately concerned with the refutation of scepticism in both science and ethics, and to have developed a theory of knowledge which rivalled that of Descartes in its importance for the formation of modern philosophy.

Also available in Past Masters:

Spinoza Roger Scruton
Bach Denis Arnold
Machiavelli Quentin Skinner
Darwin Jonathan Howard

PAST MASTERS

General Editor: Keith Thomas

Past Masters is a series of authoritative studies that introduce students and general readers alike to the thought of leading intellectual figures of the past whose ideas still influence many aspects of modern life.

'This Oxford University Press series continues on its encyclopaedic way ... One begins to wonder whether any intelligent person can afford not to possess the whole series.' *Expository Times*

KIERKEGAARD

Patrick Gardiner

Søren Kierkegaard (1813–55), one of the most original thinkers of the nineteenth century, wrote widely on religious, philosophical, and literary themes. But his idiosyncratic manner of presenting some of his leading ideas initially obscured their fundamental import.

This book shows how Kierkegaard developed his views in emphatic opposition to prevailing opinions, including certain metaphysical claims about the relation of thought to existence. It describes his reaction to the ethical and religious theories of Kant and Hegel, and it also contrasts his position with doctrines currently being advanced by men like Feuerbach and Marx. Kierkegaard's seminal diagnosis of the human condition, which emphasizes the significance of individual choice, has arguably been his most striking philosophical legacy, particularly for the growth of existentialism. Both that and his arresting but paradoxical conception of religious belief are critically discussed, Patrick Gardiner concluding this lucid introduction by indicating salient ways in which they have impinged on contemporary thought.

Also available in Past Masters:

PHILOSOPHY IN OXFORD PAPERBACKS

Ranging from authoritative introductions in the Past Masters and OPUS series to in-depth studies of classical and modern thought, the Oxford Paperbacks' philosophy list is one of the most provocative and challenging available.

THE GREAT PHILOSOPHERS

Bryan Magee

Beginning with the death of Socrates in 399, and following the story through the centuries to recent figures such as Bertrand Russell and Wittgenstein, Bryan Magee and fifteen contemporary writers and philosophers provide an accessible and exciting introduction to Western philosophy and its greatest thinkers.

Bryan Magee in conversation with:

A. J. Ayer	John Passmore
Michael Ayers	Anthony Quinton
Miles Burnyeat	John Searle
Frederick Copleston	Peter Singer
Hubert Dreyfus	J. P. Stern
Anthony Kenny	Geoffrey Warnock
Sidney Morgenbesser	Bernard Williams
Martha Nussbaum	

'Magee is to be congratulated . . . anyone who sees the programmes or reads the book will be left in no danger of believing philosophical thinking is unpractical and uninteresting.' Ronald Hayman, *Times Educational Supplement*

'one of the liveliest, fast-paced introductions to philosophy, ancient and modern that one could wish for' *Universe*

Also by Bryan Magee in Oxford Paperbacks:

Men of Ideas
Aspects of Wagner 2/e

OPUS

General Editors: Walter Bodmer, Christopher Butler,
Robert Evans, John Skorupski

A HISTORY OF WESTERN PHILOSOPHY

This series of OPUS books offers a comprehensive and up-to-date survey of the history of philosophical ideas from earliest times. Its aim is not only to set those ideas in their immediate cultural context, but also to focus on their value and relevance to twentieth-century thinking.

CLASSICAL THOUGHT

Terence Irwin

Spanning over a thousand years from Homer to Saint Augustine, *Classical Thought* encompasses a vast range of material, in succinct style, while remaining clear and lucid even to those with no philosophical or Classical background.

The major philosophers and philosophical schools are examined—the Presocratics, Socrates, Plato, Aristotle, Stoicism, Epicureanism, Neoplatonism; but other important thinkers, such as Greek tragedians, historians, medical writers, and early Christian writers, are also discussed. The emphasis is naturally on questions of philosophical interest (although the literary and historical background to Classical philosophy is not ignored), and again the scope is broad—ethics, the theory of knowledge, philosophy of mind, philosophical theology. All this is presented in a fully integrated, highly readable text which covers many of the most important areas of ancient thought and in which stress is laid on the variety and continuity of philosophical thinking after Aristotle.

Also available in the History of Western Philosophy series:

The Rationalists   John Cottingham
Continental Philosophy since 1750   Robert C. Solomon
The Empiricists   R. S. Woolhouse

POLITICS IN OXFORD PAPERBACKS

Oxford Paperbacks offers incisive and provocative studies of the political ideologies and institutions that have shaped the modern world since 1945.

GOD SAVE ULSTER!

The Religion and Politics of Paisleyism

Steve Bruce

Ian Paisley is the only modern Western leader to have founded his own Church and political party, and his enduring popularity and success mirror the complicated issues which continue to plague Northern Ireland. This book is the first serious analysis of his religious and political careers and a unique insight into Unionist politics and religion in Northern Ireland today.

Since it was founded in 1951, the Free Presbyterian Church of Ulster has grown steadily; it now comprises some 14,000 members in fifty congregations in Ulster and ten branches overseas. The Democratic Unionist Party, formed in 1971, now speaks for about half of the Unionist voters in Northern Ireland, and the personal standing of the man who leads both these movements was confirmed in 1979 when Ian R. K. Paisley received more votes than any other member of the European Parliament. While not neglecting Paisley's 'charismatic' qualities, Steve Bruce argues that the key to his success has been his ability to embody and represent traditional evangelical Protestantism and traditional Ulster Unionism.

'original and profound . . . I cannot praise this book too highly.'
Bernard Crick, *New Society*

Also in Oxford Paperbacks:

Freedom Under Thatcher   Keith Ewing and Conor Gearty
Strong Leadership   Graham Little
The Thatcher Effect   Dennis Kavanagh and Anthony Seldon

MUSIC IN OXFORD PAPERBACKS

Whether your taste is classical or jazz, the Oxford Paperbacks range of music books is in tune with the interests of all music lovers.

ESSAYS ON MUSICAL ANALYSIS
Donald Tovey

Tovey's Essays are the most famous works of musical criticism in the English language. For acuteness, common sense, clarity, and wit they are probably unequalled, and they make ideal reading for anyone interested in the classical music repertory.

CHAMBER MUSIC

Chamber Music contains some of Tovey's most important essays, including those on Bach's 'Goldberg' Variations and *Art of Fugue*, and on key works by Haydn, Mozart, Beethoven, Schumann, Chopin, and Brahms.

CONCERTOS AND CHORAL WORKS

Concertos and Choral Works contains nearly all the concertos in the standard repertory, from Bach's for two violins to Walton's for viola—fifty concertos in all. The choral works include long essays on Bach's B minor Mass and Beethoven's Mass in D, amongst other famous works.

SYMPHONIES AND OTHER ORCHESTRAL WORKS

Symphonies and Other Orchestral Works contains 115 essays: on Beethoven's overtures and symphonies (including Tovey's famous study of the Ninth Symphony), all Brahms's overtures and symphonies, and many other works by composers from Bach to Vaughan Williams.

Also in Oxford Paperbacks:

Singers and the Song   Gene Lees
The Concise Oxford Dictionary of Music 3/e
Michael Kennedy
Opera Anecdotes   Ethan Mordden

LAW FROM OXFORD PAPERBACKS

Oxford Paperbacks's law list ranges from introductions to the English legal system to reference books and in-depth studies of contemporary legal issues.

INTRODUCTION TO ENGLISH LAW
Tenth Edition

William Geldart
Edited by D. C. M. Yardley

'Geldart' has over the years established itself as a standard account of English law, expounding the body of modern law as set in its historical context. Regularly updated since its first publication, it remains indispensable to student and layman alike as a concise, reliable guide.

Since publication of the ninth edition in 1984 there have been important court decisions and a great deal of relevant new legislation. D. C. M. Yardley, Chairman of the Commission for Local Administration in England, has taken account of all these developments and the result has been a considerable rewriting of several parts of the book. These include the sections dealing with the contractual liability of minors, the abolition of the concept of illegitimacy, the liability of a trade union in tort for inducing a person to break his/her contract of employment, the new public order offences, and the intent necessary for a conviction of murder.

Other law titles:

Freedom Under Thatcher: Civil Liberties in Modern Britain
Keith Ewing and Conor Gearty
Doing the Business   Dick Hobbs
Judges   David Pannick
Law and Modern Society   P. S. Atiyah

HISTORY IN OXFORD PAPERBACKS

Oxford Paperbacks' superb history list offers books on a wide range of topics from ancient to modern times, whether general period studies or assessments of particular events, movements, or personalities.

THE STRUGGLE FOR
THE MASTERY OF EUROPE 1848–1918

A. J. P. Taylor

The fall of Metternich in the revolutions of 1848 heralded an era of unprecedented nationalism in Europe, culminating in the collapse of the Hapsburg, Romanov, and Hohenzollern dynasties at the end of the First World War. In the intervening seventy years the boundaries of Europe changed dramatically from those established at Vienna in 1815. Cavour championed the cause of *Risorgimento* in Italy; Bismarck's three wars brought about the unification of Germany; Serbia and Bulgaria gained their independence courtesy of the decline of Turkey—'the sick man of Europe'; while the great powers scrambled for places in the sun in Africa. However, with America's entry into the war and President Wilson's adherence to idealistic internationalist principles, Europe ceased to be the centre of the world, although its problems, still primarily revolving around nationalist aspirations, were to smash the Treaty of Versailles and plunge the world into war once more.

A. J. P. Taylor has drawn the material for his account of this turbulent period from the many volumes of diplomatic documents which have been published in the five major European languages. By using vivid language and forceful characterization, he has produced a book that is as much a work of literature as a contribution to scientific history.

'One of the glories of twentieth-century writing.' *Observer*

Also in Oxford Paperbacks:

Portrait of an Age: Victorian England   G. M. Young
Germany 1866–1945   Gorden A. Craig
The Russian Revolution 1917–1932   Sheila Fitzpatrick
France 1848–1945   Theodore Zeldin

OPUS

General Editors: Walter Bodmer, Christopher Butler, Robert Evans, John Skorupski

OPUS is a series of accessible introductions to a wide range of studies in the sciences and humanities.

METROPOLIS

Emrys Jones

Past civilizations have always expressed themselves in great cities, immense in size, wealth, and in their contribution to human progress. We are still enthralled by ancient cities like Babylon, Rome, and Constantinople. Today, giant cities abound, but some are pre-eminent. As always, they represent the greatest achievements of different cultures. But increasingly, they have also been drawn into a world economic system as communications have improved.

Metropolis explores the idea of a class of supercities in the past and in the present, and in the western and developing worlds. It analyses the characteristics they share as well as those that make them unique; the effect of technology on their form and function; and the problems that come with size—congestion, poverty and inequality, squalor—that are sobering contrasts to the inherent glamour and attraction of great cities throughout time.

Also available in OPUS:

The Medieval Expansion of Europe   J. R. S. Phillips
Metaphysics: The Logical Approach   José A. Benardete
The Voice of the Past 2/e   Paul Thompson
Thinking About Peace and War   Martin Ceadel

RELIGION AND THEOLOGY FROM
OXFORD PAPERBACKS

The Oxford Paperbacks's religion and theology list offers the most balanced and authoritative coverage of the history, institutions, and leading figures of the Christian churches, as well as providing in-depth studies of the world's most important religions.

MICHAEL RAMSEY
A Life

Owen Chadwick

Lord Ramsey of Canterbury, Archbishop of Canterbury from 1961 to 1974, and one of the best-loved and most influential churchmen of this century, died on 23 April 1988.

Drawing on Dr Ramsey's private papers and free access to the Lambeth Palace archive, Owen Chadwick's biography is a masterly account of Ramsey's life and works. He became Archbishop of Canterbury as Britain entered an unsettled age. At home he campaigned politically against racialism and determined to secure justice and equality for immigrants. In Parliament he helped to abolish capital punishment and to relax the laws relating to homosexuality. Abroad he was a stern opponent of apartheid, both in South Africa and Rhodesia. In Christendom at large he promoted a new spirit of brotherhood among the churches, and benefited from the ecumenism of Popes John XXIII and Paul VI, and the leaders of the Orthodox Churches of Eastern Europe.

Dr Ramsey emerges from this book as a person of much prayer and rock-like conviction, who in an age of shaken belief and pessimism was an anchor of faith and hope.

Other religion and theology titles:

John Henry Newman: A Biography   Ian Ker
John Calvin   William Bouwsma
A History of Heresy   David Christie-Murray
The Wisdom of the Saints   Jill Haak Adels

WOMEN'S STUDIES FROM
OXFORD PAPERBACKS

Ranging from the *A–Z of Women's Health* to *Wayward Women: A Guide to Women Travellers*, Oxford Paperbacks cover a wide variety of social, medical, historical, and literary topics of particular interest to women.

DESTINED TO BE WIVES
The Sisters of Beatrice Webb
Barbara Caine

Drawing on their letters and diaries, Barbara Caine's fascinating account of the lives of Beatrice Webb and her sisters, the Potters, presents a vivid picture of the extraordinary conflicts and tragedies taking place behind the respectable façade which has traditionally characterized Victorian and Edwardian family life.

The tensions and pressures of family life, particularly for women; the suicide of one sister; the death of another, probably as a result of taking cocaine after a family breakdown; the shock felt by the older sisters at the promiscuity of their younger sister after the death of her husband are all vividly recounted. In all the crises they faced, the sisters formed the main network of support for each other, recognizing that the 'sisterhood' provided the only security in a society which made women subordinate to men, socially, legally, and economically.

Other women's studies titles:

A–Z of Women's Health   Derek Llewellyn-Jones
'Victorian Sex Goddess': Lady Colin Campbell and the Sensational Divorce Case of 1886   G. H. Fleming
Wayward Women: A Guide to Women Travellers
Jane Robinson
Catherine the Great: Life and Legend   John T. Alexander